Advance Praise for *Classroom Confidential*

"I wish I had the advice from *Classroom Confidential* when I was a first year teacher. Mrs. Lucido wonderfully describes the realities of the teaching profession ranging from staff lounge conversations to eating in the classroom. These aspects weren't taught in teacher preparation school yet must be discussed and understood before you step foot into your own classroom in order to be an effective, happy, and sane teacher! The transparency of the many facets of a teacher's school life and identity, combined with advice on how to handle various situations, will help any teacher add to their "bag of tricks." While I am still amazed Mrs. Lucido survived 33 years teaching in public schools, I now understand the personality, outlook, and drive that kept her, and many others, happily in the teaching profession for so long. Regardless if you're a first or tenth year teacher, *Classroom Confidential* offers insight and tips to navigate your next school year. Thank you,

Mrs. Lucido, for impacting so many students' lives and helping myself and so many others navigate this profession!"

—Kimberly Kellam,
Academic Coach, Walter Colton Middle School

"Vickie Lucido has seen it all over her 33 year teaching career and shares her experiences with humor and wit to help prepare you for teaching in ways other teaching books do not. In *Classroom Confidential*, you'll find answers to questions that you never knew you had, but are essential to your success and longevity as a teacher. Have you ever considered how to handle an angry mom? Or how to prepare for a room full of tired parents on Back to School night? Or how to ride the storm when budget cuts and pink slips are on the horizon? *Classroom Confidential* is a quick and essential read for new and experienced teachers alike with straightforward tips for succeeding in what is a very challenging profession."

—Marianne Hartfelt,
Art Teacher, Monterey High School

Classroom Confidential

VICTORIA LUCIDO

Classroom Confidential

How I Survived 33 Years in a Public School Classroom ...and You Can Too!

NEW YORK

LONDON • NASHVILLE • MELBOURNE • VANCOUVER

Classroom Confidential

How I Survived 33 Years in a Public School Classroom...and You Can Too!

Published in New York, New York, by Morgan James Publishing. Morgan James is a trademark of Morgan James, LLC. www.MorganJamesPublishing.com

ISBN 9781642799040 paperback
ISBN 9781642799057 eBook
Library of Congress Control Number: 2019953722

Cover & Interior Design by:
Christopher Kirk
www.GFSstudio.com

Morgan James is a proud partner of Habitat for Humanity Peninsula and Greater Williamsburg. Partners in building since 2006.

Get involved today! Visit
MorganJamesPublishing.com/giving-back

For my Walter Colton Middle School Family.
We fought, we laughed, and we cried together.
I will forever be a Colton Colt.

Table of Contents

L OOK, I DON'T WANT TO TELL YOU HOW TO READ THIS BOOK or anything, but if I were you, I'd skip to the chapter about how to train your administrator and read that first. Now, I'd normally never tell a teacher to do this. It's deplorable and bizarre advice to be issued in the world of administration. How can an administrator suggest that they become trained by teachers?

But in this book, we have a unique situation because (a) Vickie was successful in training multiple administrators and (b) I was one of them so who better to tell you how she did it than me?

It's strange to think that I've only known Vickie for about five years and was her administrator for only the first three. It genuinely feels like 20. Time has zipped by since we met at my first staff meeting in the cafeteria on that cold and foggy Monterey summer morning. I was an experienced middle school principal, and I had just moved to the area and accepted an assistant principal position to be closer to my aging parents. I remember seeing her moving quickly into the room with a polished look and obviously ready to get this meeting over with and get back to her classroom. Immediately following the morning meeting, she flew out of the crowd of teachers running toward me. *Was she running?* That may be an embellishment. From the first time I met Vickie, I knew she would challenge my leadership skills. She introduced herself and began explaining her chosen responsibilities on campus and what my responsibilities would be to support her. The point is, I was intrigued.

Throughout the day, I spent time getting to know everyone, and the straight facts from everyone were that Vickie Lucido was dedicated to the culture of the school and the students and teachers within its walls. She had been on campus longer than anyone and had built celebrated traditions that were admired district-wide. Teachers explained to me that one of their favorite traditions was the Singing Telegrams that Vickie sold as a fundraiser for her drama club, and how every year the drama students traveled around campus singing in offices and classrooms the day before spring break. *What? A lost instructional day? What has the principal been thinking?* It wasn't until I witnessed the excitement of the day, and I saw the positive transformation of the culture on campus, that I began to see the value of what Vickie Lucido had created at this middle school.

Soon after spring break, I became the fifth principal of our school that year. Vickie and I had developed a strong relationship by this time, and she continued to prove to me her dedication and value to our school. When she made an appointment to meet with me, I was anticipating an update on the end-of-the-year events. Vickie talks briefly about this in the book, but I was astounded. She wanted to be excused from staff meetings and collaboration days so she could rehearse with her students for the school play. *What? NO WAY!* I really had to think this one through. Vickie had proven herself over and over again throughout the year, other staff knew the work she did, and the whole district raved about how professional her drama productions were. And, after all, I hadn't seen one of her drama productions yet. I anticipated grumbling from the other teachers, but I agreed as long as she got notes from the meetings or met with me to get the information she missed. There were no teacher complaints and the drama production was INCREDIBLE!

Vickie Lucido has all of the qualities of a superstar. Every story she tells is a performance, and every time we parted after meeting about one of her requests, whether it ended in her favor or not, she gave me a big hug. She embodies passion and most importantly, genuineness.

Now that I'm thinking about it, you should probably read this book exactly the way Vickie wrote it, with the ending thoughts at the end. She really has provided novice teachers with some valuable and somewhat uncommon advice. Take in her personal stories. Learn about her background and drive. Read how she did the work, gained the trust and respect, had the courage to tell her truth, and then schooled her administrators in how they could best support her work that supported the culture they led.

This book isn't just another teacher induction manual. It's the work of a seasoned teacher who had the presence of mind, while teaching in the trenches, to take notes and write her own version of how to succeed.

It's a drama plot come to life. After years of difficult, challenging, and just enough reward to keep her going, work, a teacher obsessed with trying her hardest to do a good job under sometimes unconceivable circumstances, gets the satisfaction of sharing her story and the lessons she has learned. Who doesn't want to read that immediately?

Good teachers are driven, diligent, collaborative, and authentic. They inspire kids and other teachers. They spend hundreds of their own personal hours and dollars doing a better job than for what they are compensated, and they care. They care about their students, their teacher colleagues, their school staff, and even their administrators. They are passionate, dedicated to their school and the lives they impact, and they fight for what they believe. It's noble work. And this book is about the lessons learned throughout a career dedicated to that work.

Janet Mikkelsen
Retired Middle School Principal

Introduction

As a retired public school teacher of 33 years, it is my desire my experience can help other teachers. Much of what happens in the classroom, no one teaches you in school. Much of what you learn is while on the job. Once you get into your classroom as a new teacher, there isn't a lot of help available since other working teachers are so busy. When I first started teaching in 1985, I was in a bit of shock. Having 30+ faces staring at me six periods a day was a bit overwhelming. I wasn't sure how to plan for an entire period and keep them busy until the bell rang. It reminded me of a Burt Reynold's movie I watched in the 80's called "Starting Over." He went into his high school classroom at 9:00 for his first day of teaching and talked for what seemed like a really long time. He said, "Well, I guess that's it for today."

A student replied, "Mr. Potter, it's only 9:05."

I felt like that at times when I first started teaching.

As I said, there wasn't much support in 1985. I went to the head teacher and asked her if I could spend some time talking to her because I was feeling lost. Her reply? "When in doubt, punt." I think her comment stemmed from some jealousy because she clearly didn't want this "young fresh-faced teacher" to be more popular than she. When I first started teaching, I witnessed a lot of competition among teachers, but I haven't seen that in my last many years of teaching. Due to that comment my first year of teaching, I had been an open door to helping other teachers.

Slowly, I found my way. Much of teaching is on-the-job training. You can work with a mentor-teacher for a long time, but until you get into your own classroom with students looking to you and you alone, you can't really start developing your own tool box of strategies.

I saw many teachers come and go. Some just weren't cut out for the job. Some realized it and did something else, others stuck with it for years when maybe they shouldn't. I always believed the best teachers have "with-it-ness." They see what needs to be done and they figure out how to do it. However, I have also seen people grow into teaching. There's no one way to be in the classroom, but there are some dos and don'ts that at least need to be considered. Mainly this book is about those dos and don'ts.

While reading this book, you may think, "Geez, did she even like being a teacher?" Let me say from the get-go, I loved being a teacher in so many ways. I was not a born teacher like some. I went to school wanting to be in performing arts, but having to work to put myself through college, I could not major in a degree requiring endless hours of rehearsal and performance.

My degree in English allowed me to teach both English and drama. Since I didn't have the thick skin to be an actress, I sort of fell into teaching. And while I never saw myself as a born teacher, as I said, I do believe it was what I was meant to do. I ended up teaching English for 20 years until the powers-that-be decided to combine English and social studies into the same period. Later, it would be separate classes of social studies and English, until my schedule morphed into no English and several periods of social studies. I taught drama my entire teaching career. I also taught leadership. One principal even asked me to teach physical education. I said I would do it for one year on an emergency credential. She found someone else to do it.

Back to my point of you possibly thinking I didn't like teaching after some of the things in this book. Teaching is a hard gig. It takes a lot of out of you, maybe *everything* out of you at times. When you go into teaching, you may think, like I did, "I'm going to change the world! I'm going to inspire young minds! I'm going to share my love of learning and create lifelong learners!" And then reality hits you like a ton of bricks.

It's the first day of school, and you are all dressed up and excited. You ask the students to share their names, and one kid tells you to call him Cat Woman. It's the first unit and you're so excited to share your travels to Mexico and show pictures of the Mayan ruins, and all a kid has to say is, "Your first name is Vickie?" when they notice the captions on the pictures you're showing, so you go in and change all of the captions omitting your first name. You're lecturing about something really important to you, like elephants in Africa, and a student raises his hand. You get excited thinking he will ask about the elephants, but instead asks, "What time does this class get out for lunch?"

Basically, kids are kids whether it's 1985 or present day. They're going to tell you what's on their mind; they are worried about having friends, they're going to act out, and they're going to behave like kids. It's what I loved about teaching the most; there's nothing fake about kids. Kids are real. And when you're real with them, you can succeed, you can connect, and you can change lives. I didn't connect with every student I encountered, but I know for a fact I have made a difference with many students because they have told me. They have written to me, and they have honored me. And for those I haven't been able to reach, there is quite possibly another teacher who has been able to break through. That's the beauty of teaching; it truly does take a village.

It is my desire you can get some helpful tips from the experiences and ideas I am sharing in this book. As a seasoned teacher, young teachers would often come to me in a panic about something happening at school. I used to panic too, but as the years went by, I learned to relax and how to cope.

As teachers, we are in the helping profession. Whenever I would get frustrated with the bureaucracy of teaching, my husband would say, "Why don't you all go on strike?" I would remind him we're not the teamsters! We're not Jimmy Hoffa! We're teachers! (Although, since the writing of this book, some school districts have resorted to striking. The district I worked for never has). This book is about how to survive the craziness and complications of our profession. I only taught in California, but from attending workshops in other states as well as knowing people who have taught in other states, I believe my book has something to offer anyone who is employed as an educator. Experienced teachers who've been in the business for a while know how to survive and how to make things work.

This book is about sharing many of my survival secrets.

Dress the Part

I'm going to start this chapter with a personal story to illustrate my point about dressing the part.

When teaching social studies, I studied about all of the ancient civilizations. While teaching about China or Africa or Rome or wherever in our book, I would think, "I want to go and see these places," and so I made it my goal to travel to each and every civilization.

The first time I went to Rome, I had no idea how to dress. My husband and I went to a travel store and purchased a lot of travel clothes. When we got to Rome, I realized we looked like Indiana Jones or someone out of an African safari. We were wearing safari type pants and shirts. I didn't adequately research what to wear and actually didn't even know I needed to. Once, while walking along Piazza Navona, a restaurant hawker called out to us, "Hey, people from California, come to our restaurant!" Obviously, the Italians could spot Americans a mile away, especially the way we were dressed!

After that trip, I made it my goal to find out what the people in the country we were planning on visiting were wearing, and my husband and I did our best to assimilate into the culture. For example, when we went to Istanbul, I didn't try to pretend to be Muslim by covering my head, still I did my best to show respect by dressing modestly. In Italy, we never wore safari clothes again. We wore beige, black, and subtle colors, and definitely NO white tennis shoes!

When we dressed more like the culture, we were treated better by the people in the country. They were more welcoming and spent more time talking to us. Some locals would even speak Italian to my husband thinking he was from Italy.

I told my students this story, and several said another teacher told them when he traveled to foreign lands he wore whatever he wanted. He actually wore what I call the American male uniform: cargo shorts, a T-shirt with some sort of writing on it, tennis shoes and socks, and a baseball cap. I tried to be polite when I said this, but I did tell the students it's true a person can wear whatever they want, but what they wear has a huge effect on how people treat and even respect you.

How does this story tie into teaching?

Depending on the district, your school may have very loose dress code rules for teachers. At my school teachers could wear just about whatever they wanted as long as the women didn't dress in a way too revealing. They could wear jeans, shorts, yoga pants, sweatshirts and other casual items of clothing. Dressing too casually can be a major problem.

I spent a lot of time thinking about what I was going to wear to school, and I believe it made a huge difference how I was treated and respected by students. I particularly spent a lot of thought on my first day of school outfit. The students' initial glimpse of you is paramount to your success for the entire year. Carefully selecting an outfit which was business-like but also feminine was very important to me. I wanted to send the message I was there to teach, and still was approachable. The first month of school I wore only skirts, dresses, or slacks with pumps or boots. In fact, when I retired in June of 2018, I was having a hard time and joked with our School Office Supervisor it was either retirement or working until I dropped dead. She joked, "I can just see you now, Mrs. Lucido, 70 years old and clicking by in your heels."

Many young teachers complain the students are not being respectful to them. They say students speak to them as if they are their peer. I advise them to consider what they are wearing. If they are dressed in jeans and a sweatshirt, this may be a reason the students are not taking them seriously.

I felt sad at one point because we had a young teacher who was wearing slacks and a tie every day and looked so professional. He taught physical education and social studies. Another teacher said to him, "You don't have to dress so nice every day! You can just wear the physical education clothes to school for all of your classes." After that, he wore sweats to school and hardly even shaved. He started having problems with discipline he wasn't having before, and I gently offered it may be because of how he is now dressing.

Just like my beginning story with travel, unless some rules prohibit it, you can dress however you like, but there are consequences to dressing too casually. If teachers want to be treated as the professionals they are, they need to dress like professionals. Would we have confidence in a lawyer or doctor who was wearing shorts and a sweatshirt to meetings?

Some young teachers have expressed financial concerns about buying more professional clothes for school. I would tell them there are many stores where you can buy inexpensive dresses or slacks. When I first started teaching, I even went to secondhand stores to find appropriate school clothes and found some of my favorite things I own.

The message here is if you want to be treated as a professional and if you want students to take you seriously, dress the part!

The Staff Lounge
Fitting In

You may think that the staff lounge is no big deal and for some people it may not be. For me, and many others, how one is welcomed by other teachers in the staff lounge is an indication of the social climate at the school. I put this chapter toward the beginning of the book to give ideas for feeling comfortable as soon as possible at your school. Some people never step foot into the staff lounge at break or lunch because they don't feel welcome. If you would like to join in the fun in the staff lounge, my experience can help you understand some of the dynamics at play. I also offer some tips for fitting in.

Teachers are generally social creatures and often reflect the age group they have chosen to teach. I worked with elementary, middle school, and high school teachers and found each group to be a different animal altogether. These differences tie into the group dynamic which in turn ties into the school gathering place: the staff lounge.

When I started out, after my student teaching in a high school and before a short stint as a high school summer school teacher, I was a substitute. Being a substitute, unless you always sub at the same school and are a known commodity, is like being a pariah. No one knows what to say to you beyond, "Who ya subbing for?" If that! When you walk into the lounge and see a sub at your regular table, you quickly plop your stuff at a different table to avoid the work it takes to make conversation with someone you don't know, even if the person seems "normal."

When I was a sub, people completely ignored me. Apparently I was absolutely invisible to the naked eye. I thought I looked normal. I was a healthy young 27-year-old who dressed as professionally as possible and behaved in a way that was not intrusive or strange, and yet every teacher who entered the lounge completely ignored me. They all gathered together talking about school or their lives as I sat there waiting for the lunch period to end.

As I became a teacher, I got it. The time in the lounge is OUR time. Our time to unwind, vent, relax, and recharge for the afternoon ahead. We have been taking care of others all day, and we don't want to take care of someone on our lunch break! Because of being a sub myself and knowing how horrible it was, I attempted to have a bit of a conversation around the microwave with a sub beyond, "Who ya subbing for?" Of course, only if the person was "normal." I don't mean to be cruel, but it was hard to imagine where some of our subs came from. Some were downright incompetent!

Subs aren't the only people in the lounge who can be difficult to endure. What about teachers with whom you work? It can also be a challenge.

Teachers can be cliquey. When I first started teaching at the middle school level, there was a group of teachers who were a definite clique. They had "their" table, and you better not sit there. It had a table cloth and candle on it and heaven help a sub if they happened to sit there. They would be shunned and so would any regular teacher who deigned to think they were welcome. You would quickly see you were not welcome by the fact no one would talk to you, or look at you. They would be talking about a party they just had or were going to have and you were definitely not invited!

One by one those teachers retired or left and I never saw the likes of a clique like that at our school again, but I did see hints of it with certain teachers sitting together with their backs to others.

When we were a Kindergarten-Eight school, the elementary teachers seldom came into the staff lounge. They often kept their classrooms open to students. We had three lunches: One for the kindergarten (which was basically five minutes after school started!) One was for the first thru sixth graders, and one for the seven/eight. If you were a seven/eight teacher and got stuck at the elementary grade lunch, it was a lonely lunch period. Hardly anyone would come in and you would sit there waiting for it to end.

The seven/eight lunch was like a lively party. Most of upper grade teachers wanted to get the heck out of their classrooms for a while and be with other teachers. Some teachers would stick together and a person could feel excluded. Once, the principal made the mistake of thinking she would be welcome in the lounge during the teachers' lunch, so she could get to know us better. Conversation came to a standstill while she was in there, even though we actually liked her! Once again, this was OUR time and we didn't want to worry about what we were saying. It was like Vegas. What's said in the staff lounge stays in the staff lounge!

I only taught at the high school for student teaching, summer school, and substitute teaching, but I have been told the high school teachers in our district are very exclusive with their departments. No one goes in the lounge, and everyone meets with their departments in someone's classroom by invitation.

Since my experience was mostly with the Seven/Eight grade lunch, here is how I survived:

I was friendly to all who entered: The first thing I did was to be friendly to everyone. Yep, even the subs. I made a point to invite newcomers to sit with the other teachers and me.

No more separate tables: Next I put the tables together so no one had their back to anyone else. With the tables together, all people felt included. True, some cliques might be at one end of the table, but it still felt better than three separate tables where there may be eight people crowded into one table, two people left out at another table, and a lonely sub sitting alone at a third table.

I worked on Hearts and Flowers (our social club): I found the other teachers like me who wanted to connect. We were in charge of birthday shout-outs, wedding and baby showers, and other celebrations.

Treat Day: We had a sign where staff signed up to bring treats at the end of each month for everyone who came into the lounge. It was always the last Friday before payday. Everyone was usually in a good mood, and the treats brought people in I seldom saw inside the lounge.

Bring treats when it's not treat day: I would often make a banana bread or cookies for no special occasion. Some people would buy donuts or coffee. When you walk into the staff lounge and see an unexpected treat, it boosts your spirits.

Bottom Line: The teachers' lounge can make you feel like you're a kid at school looking for lunch friends all over again. Try not to give up if you are feeling left out. I guarantee you there are others who are also feeling left out and would appreciate you finding a way to make everyone feel included. You are spending a lot of time at work. It is your home away from home; put some energy into creating a community for yourself and others.

Build Community

B eing a teacher is being part of a community in a way unlike other jobs I had. I worked in a bank for years, and while I enjoyed the people I worked with, I did not feel the same connection with them I did as a teacher. First of all, money is not a major focus in teaching like it is in other lines of work. There isn't quite the hierarchy as is in a bank with the branch manager on down to the tellers. True, teachers do have administrators, but they are only on a slightly higher playing ground than the teachers, whereas, in a bank, there seemed to be a wide canyon between the tellers and the bank presidents.

Another aspect of teaching different than other jobs, is we are a visible part of the community at large in a way no other career is. We are a part of people's lives that is deeply impactful, and one of the things which makes teaching so rewarding. By the time I retired, I had many children of former students as my students. I had cousins, aunts, uncles, and siblings of former students. I can barely go anywhere in town where I don't see one of my former students or the parents of former students. Being a teacher really connects you to the community outside of the classroom.

But what about the community at school? For most people, feeling a sense of belonging at the school site is essential for happiness in the teaching day. The more the staff feels connected to each other, the happier everyone is, and feeling connected helps create loyalty to your school.

Here are some ideas for creating community:

Welcome everyone into the staff lounge. I wrote an entire chapter about this because it's so important.

Happy Hours: Have regular happy hours at a nearby restaurant where everyone is invited. If the location is too far away, many people may not attend.

Staff parties at the end of the semester: We have had some great parties, and it is a time when we can all let down our guard, talk, and laugh. They can be held at a restaurant or someone's home who is willing to host.

Social Committee: Have a group of people keep track of people's birthdays, host baby and wedding showers, organize the staff parties, send condolence cards, and acknowledge and celebrate other important staff-life changes.

Pay attention to people at school who may not necessarily be your friends outside of school. There are people who may become your friends at school, whom you also choose to spend time with outside of school. It's wonderful, but some people don't make those connections and may feel excluded. Make a point to pay attention to those people and include them in your school conversations. Basically, try not to let anyone feel left out.

If you do have a party or gathering outside of school with other staff members, do not mention it in front of people who are not invited. Maybe it's a small thing, but I have seen invitations to parties in people's boxes at school, but not in everyone's box. It's worth the price of stamps, or the time it takes to send a personal email, to keep a private party, private.

Along those same lines, be careful not to appear like a clique. As I said in my Staff Lounge chapter, when I first started at Colton there was a clique of teachers excluding everyone. When I left, there was another, younger, gentler, and exclusive but less so than the previous, clique forming. I would come to school and when I would go to put my initials on the sign-in sheet, I would see little hearts next to certain people's names. The first time I thought, "Whatever," but after a few times, it bothered me. I felt strongly, whatever was done at school, should be for everyone. The School Office Supervisor started putting a heart next to my name, which was so sweet of her, but the truth is, everyone needs a heart every day at school!

Some years we would do Secret Santa at school. It could be sweet or it could be hurtful. Participation in Secret Santa was completely voluntary. If you chose to participate, you were expected to put a small gift in your chosen staff member's box each day ($3.00 to $5.00 in value Monday through Thursday and up to $10.00 in value on Friday before winter break). Some people would lavish their person while some people would neglect to give the daily gifts. Some people would give used stuff they didn't want! If you're going to do a Secret Santa idea, make sure to do a good job, or you could really hurt someone's feelings.

In teaching, we don't make a lot of money, and since we're not in it for the money, small acts of kindness can keep us going from day-to-day. Be the person who makes someone else's day a little brighter; you probably won't even be aware of how much good it did!

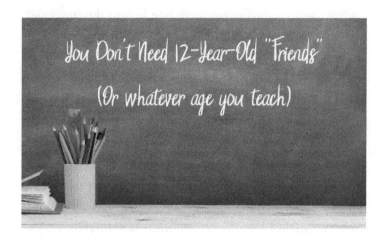

You Don't Need 12-Year-Old "Friends"
(Or whatever age you teach)

Many times I've seen new teachers (and sometimes even ones who've been around a while), make the mistake of trying to get the kids to like them by attempting to be their friend instead of establishing a more positive professional relationship. I'm similar to most teachers and want the students to enjoy being with me, but I would always choose respect over like. The beginning of the year is always fraught with excitement. Everyone is wearing their new clothes, kids have all of their new school supplies, and teachers' classrooms are spiffed up for a new and exciting year. Teachers who don't have a lot of experience may erroneously believe that this new excitement will continue all year, and they can be chummy with the kids and save the world.

WRONG!

If a teacher makes the mistake of being too cozy with kids in the beginning of the year, there may be problems when the teacher tries to actually start expecting kids to do things they may not want to do, such as homework.

It is hard to hold the line with students. In my "Dress the Part" chapter, I discussed dressing like a professional, and now I'm suggesting teachers behave like professionals. What do I mean? I mean you don't have to be stern or "mean" (the kids' word for strict), but you have to be resolute in your expectations. I have seen teachers allow the students to do things to avoid their whining, and then it backfires and their classrooms are chaos. I honestly don't know how some teachers get through the day with what is happening in their classrooms. I tell teachers, (who ask) "You can do the hard-easy thing or the easy-hard thing." Meaning, you can start out strict and then ease off as you establish control, or you can allow the students to get away with things, and then try to pull back once you've lost control, which could create a rebellion.

I personally have always chosen the hard-easy way. It takes a lot of energy at the beginning of the year to set expectations in your classroom, however, after about a month of exhausting work, you can actually teach the rest of the year.

The following are some mistakes I have seen teachers make in the beginning of the year, so kids will like them:

Allowing kids to eat in class: This is a huge mistake. Teachers have tried to justify it by saying the kids are so hungry and can't concentrate, or I have heard teachers say they are hungry, so they need to eat and let the kids eat.

Let me tell you, I have never let kids eat in my room, except for the occasional party, and every kid has survived just fine.

When they know they won't be allowed to eat in your room, guess what? They plan their time accordingly and make sure to eat before they get there. When you allow students to eat in your room, you are sending a message you don't trust them to organize their time. What you're teaching is secondary to them eating, and you don't care if your classroom is messy and smelly. Many students get very upset if a classroom smells like food. Let's face it, what they are eating is not usually healthy anyway. Not to mention others are distracted by asking the kids with food to share. Your classroom becomes a second cafeteria, and the students become less focused on learning and more on eating.

Letting kids "run around to burn off steam" before teaching them: It is a preposterous idea, yet I have heard more than one teacher think it was a good idea. Here's why it isn't: Students can be calm if it's what you expect, but if you think it's okay for them to run off steam, they will have an endless supply. Then if you say, "Okay, that's enough. Settle down." You may get a big argument about how much running around is enough for their amount of steam.

I have seen teachers try to pull back on the running around, only to get kids arguing with them and angry saying the teacher is now being mean by not allowing them to run around anymore. I have seen the same student perfectly calm in one classroom and argumentative and hyper in another classroom. The big difference is the teacher's expectations.

Allowing kids to swear in class: If you don't behave like a professional at the beginning of the year and if you want students to believe you are nice or even cool, you may wonder why in the heck kids believe they can "cuss" in your class. I'll tell you why:

It's because they think of you as more of a peer than an authority figure. There is some loss of respect for you as their teacher.

I've always believed students should have a healthy fear of their teachers. I know some students don't even respect their parents, but for those who do, and may be a little afraid of their mom or dad if they make them mad, that is how kids should feel about their teachers. They should know you care. You are not their friend. You are a caring and supportive adult, and you expect them to behave in your presence.

Allowing kids on their cell phones in class: I know I'm old school, but I think allowing kids to get on their cell phones in a classroom is flat out lazy teaching. I think it's fine if their cell phones are being used for your curriculum. For example, I allowed students to use cell phones in drama class to look up lyrics to songs for their projects. If a teacher is allowing them to use cell phones for something non-academic once they are finished with work or while they work, the teacher is asking for trouble. It's amazing how quickly a student can get work done if they are rewarded with their cell phone when they "finish."

I see cell phones as a tool you should be able to control and not control you. I believe teachers who allow students to have their cell phones out all the time and may even have their own cell phones out, are dropping the ball on their responsibilities. In my opinion, they see it as easier for them to have the students less distracting to others by being on their phone (pacifier) rather than keep students busy with their lessons. Again, they are doing the easy-hard thing because eventually, when they want the students to get off their phones, they may face a rebellion. Now they're dealing with a very "hard" situation.

Allowing students to wear hoods and hats in class: I know it's a pain to constantly be on kids about taking off their hats or lowering their hoods, but it does get easier when they know the expectation in your room. Kids hide ear buds and other things inside their hoods. Hats become a distraction when someone grabs it or doesn't like what it says on it. Plus, I try to teach boys to be gentlemen. You would never see a military man come into your room and not remove his hat. I know these kids are not in the military, however, my point: removing your hat is polite and the sign of a gentlemen. I also ask girls to remove hats. Part of our job is to teach manners in social settings.

My husband and father-in-law are very offended when they see people in restaurants sitting at a table wearing hats. Some students are probably not even aware they are offending people with their hats since maybe their parents even do it. I enjoyed being treated like a lady in my classroom. I dressed like one and I behaved like one, and I did my best to model polite behavior for my students. I would stand at the door and say, "Please take off your hat or hood. Thank you for taking off your hat or hood." Taking off hats and hoods is an example of being polite and it's also avoiding other problems that can occur in your classroom.

Allowing kids to litter or write on desks in your classroom: Your classroom is your home away from home, and the way it looks tells students everything they need to know about you. I have been in classrooms where there are entire drawings on a desk. When I mentioned it to the teacher, they may have said, "I know. It's hard to keep up with kids writing on the desks." Again, I think it's dropping the ball. I know it takes a lot of work to keep a classroom clean, but I'll tell you this, many students really appreciate it. I would often take cleaner to my desks, since my desks were clean, fewer students wrote on them. Occasionally, I would mention the writing to a student and say, "I am noticing writing on this desk. It probably isn't you (even though I thought it was), but I am monitoring it to see who it is." And guess what? The writing would magically stop!

I would check for litter each period and politely ask students to pick it up and throw it away. I would say, "You probably didn't throw the litter down, but would you please pick it up and throw it away?" More often than not, they would comply with no argument. A clean classroom shows you care. You're paying attention, and you are present in what is happening in your room.

Allowing students to chew gum: Do you really want to watch a student chewing gum? Besides the obvious mess, chewing gum can be a big distraction. I know there's research stating that students can focus better while chewing gum. Our school tried, and it lasted for about a day. Students were sticking the gum everywhere when they were finished with it, students were pestering other students for gum, and it became a major messy distraction. I also saw teachers chew gum while teaching, and it is not a pretty sight!

Allowing kids to go to the bathroom: You need to be VERY discerning about allowing kids hall passes. If you are lenient with this, you will have a revolving door in your classroom. You need to have a plan firmly in place and stick with it. I seldom allowed kids to use the bathroom. Our school said no one out the first and last ten minutes of class, and the periods were generally 50 minutes.

If a student asked and it was close to the end of the period, I would ask if they could wait. If it was a student who asked too often, I would say they could go as long as it wasn't the first or last ten minutes of the period, but they would have to give me the time back at passing period. Usually they would say they could wait. If a student asked who I completely trusted and seldom asked, I would quietly hand them the pass.

The problem is, if students think it is open season on the hall pass, one after the other will ask to leave the entire period. There were teachers who didn't follow the first and last ten minutes rule and let the students go to avoid their whining. I'm telling you the kids are not stupid! Those teachers' classrooms became the bathroom break room. Once again, like the eating situation, if students know it's a hard sell to go the bathroom from your class, they will use their passing periods. I used to tell the students, "I was nine months pregnant and didn't leave my classroom to use the bathroom. If I can wait, so can you." But, like I said, I did make exceptions when I could tell the student truly couldn't wait. And I never had any student have an "accident" in my room in 33 years of teaching.

I may come off as super strict in my classroom, and I guess I was. I ran a very tight ship. Many teachers would come into my classroom and see students calmly working and me calmly teaching, and ask, "How do you do this?" I replied I didn't really know. It just always happened this way every year, but now I'm retired, and taking the time to really think it through. I realized it was a lot of work to create a productive classroom and well worth the effort.

Seize Your Power!

Some teachers, especially new ones, may want to be too nice to students, permitting them behind their desks, or letting them use their supplies without holding them accountable for returning them, and basically allowing students too much into their personal space. The problem is if you don't have good boundaries around being "nice," the kids can exhaust the living daylights out of you! It's much harder to do the hard-easy thing than the easy-hard thing, but it's also much more effective. It's better to come in strong and ease back a bit because if you come in too nice and then pull back, you have to work a whole lot harder to gain control. (If it's even possible at all after being too lenient.).

At the beginning of the year, I used to draw the following continuum on the board:

Nice ——————————— Me ——————————— Mean

I would explain to them I will never be the extreme nice teacher who wants to be their friend and who will let them do whatever they want. I will also never be the extreme mean teacher who seems to hate kids and should get out of teaching. I am the teacher who does her best to be in the center; I will be nice enough to be a teacher who cares, and I will be mean (strict) enough to keep students accountable for their work and their behavior. However, depending on students' behavior and doing their work, I can move in either direction.

I let students know if they were not behaving, being disruptive, and not working, I would move toward the mean (strict side), and if students were behaving and getting their work done, I would move toward the nice (more fun) side. How I ran the class had a lot to do with them. I did my best to stay balanced, in the middle, remembering my job was to teach, and I never ignored bad behavior in order to push through a lesson.

I saw classrooms where the students were being rude and out of control, and yet the teacher was still allowing them privileges and trying to make it fun. I believe the teacher thought students would eventually settle down and buy into their lesson. However, it simply does not work to reward kids for misbehaving, hoping you can bribe them into behaving and then giving them way too much power. I used to think to myself, "It's going to be you or me, and it ain't gonna be me!" Meaning there was no way I was going to relinquish my power to students. I used every strategy in my teaching tool box to successfully maintain control of the classroom.

I would also explain to students I had a teacher's budget of a certain amount of money needed to last me all year. I asked them,

"What would happen if I spent all of my budget the first month of school?" Of course, the students would respond I would have no money left the rest of the year to buy anything, and it would be a long year for me. I would then tell them their behavior was like that with me. Each student had a certain amount of my patience. If a student spent it all within the first month (and on rare occasions, the first week!) of school, it would be a very long year for that student. Some students wouldn't even use up any of my patience, and they would receive "bonuses," for example, my trust to have certain privileges like taking a note to the office or helping in the classroom. Other students would not even be allowed out of their desks to sharpen their pencils until they could earn back some of my trust. Trust, meaning I felt confident they will get out of their seats to do appropriate behaviors like sharpening a pencil or tossing trash in the garbage can. They had shown they would not be using the time out of their seats to disrupt the other students with inappropriate behaviors like talking to students, passing notes, or throwing things across the room.

The most important thing to remember is you need to communicate you are in control of the classroom. Everything in your voice, your body language, your appearance, and your actions needs to convey it. You can threaten and yell at students all day long, but they will not believe you until you show them. It is much more effective to be calm, say what you mean and mean what you say. I was always the "Queen" of my classroom, and there was never any doubt to anyone as to who was in charge. Kids want to know you are in charge. They feel safe knowing you are dealing with behavior fairly and appropriately.

I would let students know there were only two things required to get along with me: Do your work and let me teach the class. If you didn't do your work or if you made it difficult for me to teach the class, we simply were not going to get along. The funny thing is I learned about myself from a student. Being a teacher at the same school for so many years, I had a reputation. One of my new students told me when she saw my name on her class schedule, she asked her cousin, a former student of mine, about me. The former student said, "To get along with Mrs. Lucido, do your homework and let her teach the class." I thought, "Out of the mouths of babes!"

I did have rules, which I refer to in other chapters, but having a million rules is not a good idea. One person I taught with had 27 rules. In my opinion, no one can remember 27 rules! I liked the "do your work and let me do mine" idea because it was so simple yet students knew what I meant. At the beginning of the year when I was informing them of my classroom expectations, I would tell them that there may come a time when they think, "Mrs. Lucido is so mean!" And I would say, "Ask yourself, 'Am I doing my work? Am I letting her teach the class? 'If you can say no to either of those questions, then you know why we are not getting along." The good news is the solution is simple: Start doing your job, let me do mine, and all will be well!

Some students may think a teacher doesn't like them, but there have been very few students in all my years of teaching who I didn't care for. Usually it was simply because I was holding the student accountable and he or she didn't appreciate it or me. I suppose no one prefers to be disliked. I always chose being respected. I knew I had to be the adult and sometimes it came with a few students not caring for me and the things I had to do in order to run the class for all students. Generally, however, most students were very respectful and did seem to like me. I think they felt safe in my class knowing I was in charge. Don't be afraid to take control of your class. Remember you are the adult in the room and the one responsible for <u>all</u> students being able to learn!

The Three B's of Teaching: Boundaries Boundaries Boundaries

ome of what I am saying in this chapter has already been said in previous chapters. I strongly believe it bears repeating. You simply will not survive in teaching if you don't have good boundaries. You have to take care of yourself because, and I can say this with a 100% guarantee, if you don't take care of yourself, no one else is going to do it. It's similar to the plane analogy where you are told to put your own oxygen mask on before assisting others. Let's face it, you can't help anyone if you pass out or are dead, and it's same with teaching. If you are ready to quit and your tank is on empty, you're not going to be able to be present in your classroom with 30+ students staring at you! Teaching is a hard job, and it requires you to be so strong. It can be exhausting! You've got to take good care of yourself if you want to survive and thrive in the classroom.

Here are some "Boundary" suggestions I found helpful:

Make sure to get enough sleep: This is not something at school, obviously, but it is essential to being able to handle the challenges at school. You simply cannot teach well if you are tired. Whatever you have to do in order to sleep, do it. If you have a stack of papers to grade, and it's getting late, put them aside, and go to sleep. Don't allow anything to get in the way of your rest. If I didn't get enough sleep, my nerves were frazzled, and I didn't do a good job being patient with students. They didn't deserve to have a teacher behaving that way. On those rare days, I would tell them, "I am so sorry. I did not get sleep last night because <u>fill in the blank</u>, and I am not doing well. It is not your fault, but please do not push me today." It seldom happened, so generally students were very compassionate.

Don't plan on them being understanding if you're tired on a regular basis. They want you to be there for them and will get resentful if you are tired every day, even if you're pregnant or with a new child; they expect you to show up and do your job.

Get Exercise: Doing something physical does wonders for your well-being. I have gone to the gym three times a week for about 30 years. NOTHING would stop me from my three times a week routine. If I had time, I would also take a walk with friends. Some teachers would say they are too busy to exercise. The benefits are so great, I would always make the time. I was rarely absent; when I retired I had 276 sick days, and it was because I always took the best care of myself I could. Exercise helped me to stay strong enough to deal with 180+ middle schoolers every single day.

Protect your personal space: Don't allow kids behind your desk or around the white board. This may sound obvious, still I have seen kids all over a teacher's space. Some students will write all over the board when the teacher's not looking. Allowing students in your space sends a message to kids you don't value yourself and it leads them to believe they have a lot of power in the classroom. You would most likely never get into their personal space, so why would you allow them into yours? I would simply tell students the first day of school they were not allowed back behind my desk, and it never became a problem.

Beware Phone Cameras: I had strict rules in my classroom regarding cell phones. They were to be put away. If a phone accidentally rang, I would politely ask them to turn it off understanding it's easy to forget your phone was left on by mistake, and it could happen to anyone, including me, so I didn't make a big deal out of it. If I saw a phone out, I would ask them nicely to put it away, and if I saw it out again, I would take it away and let them know they would have to get it from the office at the end of the day. I rarely ever had to take a student's phone away. They believed me because when I said I would do something, I did it.

As I wrote previously, occasionally in drama, I would allow students to use their phones to look up lyrics or other information tied into the lesson. I made it clear they were not to take pictures or shoot video of anything we were doing in class. I had this rule because I never wanted students to worry about something we did in class ending up on social media. I also didn't want to contend with who was okay with being filmed and who wasn't. Leaving the phones out of the equation of the drama class made life much easier, and in my opinion, safer.

When I went to Japan with students for our Junior Wings Exchange program, every time a student took pictures to post on social media, I was acutely aware of my expression and body language. Why? I'm sure you know why, but I will write about it anyway. Kids can be mean (and adults too sadly). Maybe the student taking the picture is a wonderful child, but someone else sees the picture on social media, makes a negative comment, and hurts someone's feelings. I know that social media is everywhere and it's hard to control. My feeling about bullying on social media: Not on my watch!

While we're on the subject of Social Media, be VERY careful what you post! You may think your 600+ Facebook friends are going to keep your confidence, but please think again. You don't know who among those friends have students in your class or know someone who does. I did not join social media until I retired because I didn't want anything I posted to be misconstrued. Even now, as a retired teacher, I am very careful about what I post. Remember parents and students look up to you as a role model, and you need to behave as one anywhere the public can see you.

Be careful when sharing equipment: I am all for sharing ideas, materials, and anything else that helps with teaching; however, be careful when sharing certain things. As a drama teacher, I was constantly using the stage lights and sound equipment. When I first came to Colton in 1991, the lights and sound equipment were old. The light box was archaic and all we had was an old sound box with a corded microphone. Over the years, I built the program. The drama club bought an update for the light box, and by the time I left, we had a full sound booth in the back of the cafeteria (with the stage) with several speakers, lapel mics, handheld mics, and all other equipment you would need to successfully run a middle school performance.

At first, I shared everything I used for drama with everyone, and, unfortunately, people did not care about the equipment the way I did. They would play the music too loud at a rally and blow out speakers. There was a pull down screen at the center of the stage near a hanging microphone. Several times, while I was still teaching, someone let go of the screen without guiding it. In order to close it, they would allow the screen to fly up breaking the hanging mic. People using the equipment would not turn off the stage lights properly and burn a fuse and do other things that damaged the equipment and made it hard for me to do my job.

After replacing several sets of speakers and hanging microphones, my husband, the principal, the leadership teacher, and I sat down and had a meeting. My husband agreed to set up three different sound systems for the school: a house system, a leadership system, and a drama system (he used to run a DJ business), if the drama sound system was left alone with only me having the key. My principal agreed. Just remember: No one is going to care about your property as much as you do.

Don't feel obligated to share something of value just because someone asks. If you choose to share, train the person if necessary, and make sure the person understands the expectations around what you're sharing. It may make you uncomfortable to say no, but keep in mind, if your property gets damaged, chances are you're the one who is going to have to repair or replace it. At least it's what was true for me.

Learn to say no: It is okay to say no! You don't have to say yes to every request. Teachers often feel like they have to give and give. If what is being asked of you will make it hard for you to do the job you already have, say no. What good will you be to anyone if you spread yourself too thin? Whatever you do, don't say yes when you mean no. It only leads to confusion and resentment. Be respectful. Say no when you need to.

Say yes when you know what is being asked of you: It's great to say yes; just make sure you have all of the information and know the expectations. It feels good to be singled out and asked to do something, but you may be sorry if you aren't clear on the details.

Stay as autonomous as possible: Every year my drama club would sell chocolate bars to raise money for our performance needs. Twice I was asked by people, once by the PTA and once by an afterschool program, to hand over my chocolate sales to them. Both guaranteed I would make as much money, if not more, in sales than I usually did on the chocolate bars if I gave them control over the fundraiser. I was tempted, but my husband warned me to stay autonomous. I listened to him, and I'm so glad I did. Both people ending up leaving the school, and I would have given up my main way to raise money for the drama club. If something is working, sometimes others want to come in and ride your coattails. If what you are doing is successful for you, protect it and let others find their own way. You can offer advice, only don't give away what is working for you.

Think twice before agreeing to teach summer school: If you need more money in the summer, it would be better to be a waiter, a golf caddy, or anything but a teacher. Summer is the time to refresh and rejuvenate, and if you are teaching all summer, it could be a very long school year. During the summer, it's important to do things to excite you about teaching again. One of the things I did was to travel to every civilization I taught about in seventh grade social studies. I would get so excited to go to the places I taught about in the social studies textbook, and I would be equally excited to come back and share about Africa, China, Peru, and all of the other places I traveled that were in the book. It really reenergized me. I know not everyone can or wants to travel to other lands, so find out what excites you about teaching. If you can spend some time in the summer reenergizing yourself, it will make the school year more interesting. If you spend the summer teaching, you may find yourself burned out midway through the school year.

Advocate for yourself: Don't allow anyone to stomp on you. Administrators are not "above" you; they simply have a different job description. If you feel strongly about something you need in order to be a good teacher, speak up. You may have to accept no for an answer, but at least try! You never know; sometimes you may get a yes.

I believe some of my suggestions can help you. The main thing is to always put yourself first. It is not being selfish. Everyone feels more comfortable around a person who values and takes care of themselves, and in the process you become a good role model. Taking care of yourself is essential for you to do a good job and truly be there for others.

Use Rewards Sparingly

B e careful when you use rewards in the classroom. Kids know when they are being "bought," and it doesn't make for a productive classroom. It's a lot like giving every kid a trophy just for showing up; they don't value those trophies and realize they don't deserve them. When a student is rewarded for something actually meriting a reward, you can see their face light up.

At my school, we had Colton bucks. How the bucks were used and what they would get for them upon redemption varied from year to year and from principal to principal. In my opinion, there were a lot of problems with the bucks.

One problem was how the students earned the bucks. I was giving them out when students went a week without missing doing their homework, and it was working really well for me. Unfortunately, I was told the bucks cannot be handed out for anything expected of them, such as homework; they had to be handed out if you saw students doing something random, for example, helping another student, or picking up trash without being asked. The problem with that, for me, was often when a student would do a simple kindness, he or she would look at me and ask, "Can I have a Colton buck?" I know I'm old school, but I believe students should be intrinsically motivated, and not expect to get a reward every time they do something a bit above and beyond what is expected of them.

Other problems with bucks included teachers giving out "a million" of them a day decreasing their value. Also, the prizes they could redeem them for changed so often students lost interest. At times there was no plan in place for redemption. Basically there wasn't a lot of consistency with the bucks, so they usually sat in my teacher desk forgotten.

One reward that worked in my classroom was earning a party day. If 100% of the students did their homework on any given day, they would get 5 party points. I would also give points if students all turned in their first day of school packets, Federal Emergency cards, and other school requirements. The students were motivated by the party points, and they would put pressure on each other to get their work done. Once the class reached 100 points, we would have a party with a movie and food. To me, it was a true reward. The students would be beyond excited on party day, and it created a wonderful feeling in the classroom which would extend long after the celebration had ended.

When teachers overuse rewards, it can set a bad precedent for the rest of the school. For example, I subbed on my prep period one day for a math teacher who had laid out "a billion" rewards on her desk for the students. If they raised their hand, I was supposed to give them a candy. If they finished their work, I was supposed to give them a pencil. With each student expectation met, I was supposed to give them a reward from her desk. She made up "Piggy bucks," and at the end of the quarter, she would go to the dollar store and purchase a bunch of stuff for them to buy with their Piggy bucks.

Her idea set up a negative dynamic on campus. Students started expecting to receive some sort of reward for doing basic student actions. I took one look and told students I was not going to hand out a single reward while I was subbing the class. And guess what? They had no problem accepting what I said and they went to work. I believe the students did not have a lot of respect for the teacher who freely handed out all of those rewards, even though they took them from her. They knew it wasn't right and she was "buying them" into working. Rewards should mean something. Kids aren't stupid; they know when they deserve a reward and when they don't.

I'm in no way saying not to give out rewards. I am saying the students should earn those rewards. If you are a teacher who is constantly trying to bribe your kids, you are sending a message you have run out of ideas and you don't have the confidence and conviction to manage them. I know of a teacher who could not handle class discipline the first week and was offering chocolate to the students if they would simply be quiet long enough for her to teach the lesson. She was surprised they continued to talk and didn't care about the chocolate. Of course they didn't! They had control of the teacher and the class and it is way more rewarding and exciting than a piece of chocolate! You can buy your own chocolate. Being able to get the teacher running scared and having control of the class is priceless.

Remember, whatever you do in the case of rewards should not be done out of fear of student misbehavior. Everything you do should come from a position of strength and confidence. The students know when you're in control and when you're not. Reward them when they have earned it and not when you have no idea what else you can do to control them, unless you want them to control YOU!

Your New BFFs: The Custodian and
the School Office Supervisor

The school custodian and the School Office Supervisor (formerly called the School Secretary) can make or break your career. These people truly run the school. They are the ones who you can count on to be there for you or not, depending on your relationship with them. I have seen so many administrators come and go. More often than not, the School Office Supervisor and custodians usually stick around a lot longer. I have known teachers who believe the classified staff are beneath them and think that these people are there to serve them. I can't begin to tell you what a mistake it is to believe these people are somehow below you.

Let me begin with the school custodian. My dad was an auto mechanic and handy man, so I have always had a deep appreciation for the school custodians. When I first started teaching in 1985, I worked with a man who reminded me of my father, so we got along immediately. He was a sweetheart. I thought all custodians would be like him. Unfortunately, it hasn't always been the case, but it has been close.

I left my first school because it was set to close due to the base closure. It never did end up closing, but I had already left. It was my first years at Colton where I encountered my only negative experience with a custodian. He was very territorial and a bully. Being the drama teacher, I had specific needs with the multi-use room, and it was a problem for this custodian. He didn't like me using the multi-use room, which he felt was his territory. I tried my best to get along with him; I always made sure the students and I left the room clean. There were times he wouldn't allow us to come in, so eventually I had to report him. After the talk with the principal and him, he stopped making my life difficult. If you are ever in a situation where a staff member is bullying you, by all means report it. It can be scary, especially if you're the new kid on the block. No one has the right to prevent you from doing your job just because it makes work for them they're supposed to be doing!

Other than that one person, every other custodian has been great and helpful. Our current custodian was amazing. I don't know what I would have done without him. He would always help with whatever I needed and never acted like I was imposing on him. When you have a good custodian who is there for you, it makes life pleasant and your school day go smoothly. Once the custodian who was bullying me stopped, my work life improved dramatically. Again, being a drama teacher, my needs may have been a bit more than a teacher only in the classroom. Besides cleaning my classroom like any other teacher, I would need the custodian's help to set up and take down chairs for performances, fix a sagging stage curtain, replace stage lights requiring a very tall ladder, fix wobbly prop tables, and everything else you can imagine I couldn't do myself. The most important aspect of a custodian for me was their willingness to allow me into the multi-use room with no conflict.

The School Office Supervisor (SOS) is the same exact situation. My first teaching job was with a kind and loving SOS. I relied heavily on her as a first year teacher. After her, I had others who had also been helpful, efficient, and invaluable. I often said the principal is like the mom of the school, but maybe the administrator is more like the dad, and the SOS is the mom. She's (I say "she" because I have never had a male SOS, but I imagine there are schools that have a man in this position) the one you go to with all of your problems. She's also the one who helps with any extra activities you are planning for students. True, it's ultimately up to the principal to say yes, but it's the SOS who makes it all happen.

The SOS is in charge of a myriad of duties. Her job description includes, but is not limited to, getting you the paperwork if you want to fundraise, giving you instructions and paperwork for your field trip, telling you how to utilize your Associated Student Body account if you are an elective, and helping you with all of the paperwork for your club. She will make sure your sub has what they need, and I had one SOS who called the sub service for teachers. She also gives you the paperwork if you need to take a personal day, and makes sure you get your paycheck. As the right-hand person for the administration, she may be involved in creating the testing schedule and other administrative duties. Basically, she is at the center of what is happening at school and is the all-knowing person more than anyone else on staff.

When you start teaching at a new school, one of the first things you need to do is introduce yourself to the custodian(s) and the SOS. When you speak with them, do it with respect and the understanding they are busy taking care of a lot of people. There may be days when they are short with you because there are many people demanding something from them. Be patient. And thank them! I always made sure to give thank you cards and a small gift to the people behind the scenes making my life better. I appreciated everything they did for me.

Your Classroom = Your Castle

J ust like in Feudal Europe, you can't control what goes on outside your "castle." Of course, there are obvious differences between a castle and your classroom; does your classroom belong to you? No. Does what happen in your classroom affect you? Absolutely! Your classroom is where you spend a large part of your life each day, and how it is set up can make your school day a heaven or a hell. You can't put a moat around your classroom, however, there are some things you can do to protect your "kingdom."

When the district says they are improving your classroom with updates, make sure to ask lots of questions before you allow them in. Even if you have to bar your door, do it! If you don't, it could be a long year for you in a challenging classroom.

The following are some examples:

New Desks: One year our district got a bond passed, and we were told all of the classrooms were getting new furniture.

It never occurred to me to ask who was picking out the new furniture, what it would look like, how functional it would be for my needs, or if there would be any problems with it. I had an old kind of desks. They were one big unit with the chair and desk attached and a basket underneath for books. It was sort of a Hodge podge set of desks, and I was happy with them. When I was told I was getting new desks, I assumed, quite erroneously, they would be updated versions of the desks I had.

I came back to school in August and there were the new desks. They were tables with separate chairs. We were told these desks would be great for putting kids into collaborative groups. Most teachers liked the desks. I was not happy from the minute I laid eyes on them, but I figured I could make it work. Unfortunately, there were many things about the desks that made my teaching life difficult.

Kids would lean back in the chairs, there was a bar in the front to hold the desk together and kids would stuff all sorts of garbage and food in the little front bar. I could probably have put up with all of it, except what really drove me crazy the most was there was no place for their textbooks. They had a book at home and we had a class set in the room. With the books on the desks, kids would pick at them (one student tore off all of the page numbers in the corners), and would basically destroy them by fidgeting with them. I tried handing the books out at the beginning of the period, which didn't work because not only did it take too much time, there was no accountability to who was using each book. I tried everything I could think of to solve the problem. Finally, I found out that the district had some of the old fashioned one unit desks in storage. I jumped on it, and with the help of the custodian and the facilities manager, I got my desks traded for the kind I had in the first place. I cannot tell you how much better my teaching life was after that!

New White Board: Again, I hadn't learned to ask questions. I was told I was getting a new white board, and I was excited to be getting one. At this time, I was an English and drama teacher teaching in a science classroom. I had the kind of white board with one behind and one on top to slide in front. I used both of them. When I came back to school in August, I saw they nailed the new white board on the bottom one, so I could no longer slide the top one down in front. The little shelf which held my dry erase markers was removed to be able to nail the new white board over the old one. I really needed both the top and the bottom white boards, so I ended up taking off the new white board and giving it to another teacher. Unfortunately, the shelf for my dry erase markers could not be reattached, so I had to live without it.

In my district's defense, years later when I was in a different classroom, I was told once again I would be getting a new white board. I went to my principal and told her I didn't want one because I was afraid of what happened years before in the other classroom. She said I could refuse the new white board.

Later, while walking around the school and looking in at other classrooms, I saw what great care they were taking to install the new white boards. A parent of one of our students, who also worked for the district, was doing the work, and he was doing a great job. Once I saw how wonderful the new boards looked, I went back to my principal and asked her if it was too late to get a new white board after all. Fortunately it wasn't. This time I loved my new white board!

New Heater: We had heaters in our classrooms sounding like a plane taking off. They were so loud, you had to shout over them. I brought someone in to hear what we were dealing with and was told to hook up a microphone when using the heater. However, when told they were replacing the heater in my classroom, I was skeptical. I figured my air plane sound was probably better than whatever they had in store for me with the new heater. Fortunately, I finally learned the best way for me to navigate classroom improvements. I decided to ask questions this time, and I'm so glad I did because I averted a disaster.

There were tall cabinets along my back wall, and at the very end, I had a nifty little counter with long drawers for posters underneath and two big drawers on the side necessary for supplies.

By asking questions, I found out they were planning to take out my counter unit to put in the heater. I told them I needed the counter unit. I had nowhere else to put posters, and I needed the counter top for my pencil sharpener since there were only two outlets in the entire classroom and the other one was behind my desk.

They were not happy I was fighting them on this, but I would not budge. I told them they could leave the loud heater, but they weren't taking my counter unit. They told me they could not leave the noisy heater, and unlike the new white board, I had no choice but to have a new one.

I fought and fought with them, refusing to cooperate, when finally, the head guy came out to talk to me. Exasperated, he said, "What can we do to solve this problem?"

"You can see what I'm talking about, right?" I said, "This is the only counter, the only outlet for students, and the only drawers in my classroom."

He offered, "How about if we take out one of your tall cabinets and move the counter one down? Can you do without a couple of tall cabinets?"

"Absolutely!" I exclaimed.

So by asking questions and not going blindly into the situation, I got a new quiet heater, and kept my little counter unit!

It makes me wonder about the first new white board incident. Perhaps, if I had asked questions, we could've found a way to install the board where it could've worked for me.

Remember: you are in your room A LOT and no one knows what you need better than you do. When you are told something will be done to improve your classroom, make sure you find out exactly what they mean. If it's a bad fit for you, check if you can do something to stop it, get a choice in what it is, or alter it to make it work for you. I don't like to create conflict, but it was a price I was willing to pay. I had to spend eight hours a day in my classroom, and how it's set up made all the difference to how happy and productive I was spending time in there.

The Facts About Facilities!

If you're like most people, you prefer not to be a pest. You don't want to bug people and cause them to dislike you. When it comes to dealing with the facilities department, you may have to stretch beyond your comfort zone. In the previous chapter, I wrote about what to do when the district decides to make improvements to your classroom. What about when you are asking to have something done? Well, that's a whole different ball game!

If you work in a small district with lots of money and resources, and district people who are living just to make your teaching day better, you are fortunate, and you're also in the minority. My former school district was huge, covering ten miles with 22 schools and hundreds of teachers, not to mention having many other buildings including the District Office and the Instructional Materials Center. It was very challenging to get something done in one classroom.

Here is an example:

The stage curtain caper: When I first started teaching in 1985, apparently no one was worried about fire because every stage in our district had very old, tan, ugly stage curtains. Every year, when the principal would tell us we got some magic money from somewhere and asked us to write down something we would love to have and the "sky is the limit," I would write down "new stage curtains." Of course, every year it would not happen. In fact, I don't recall anyone ever getting one of their requests off of those "dream big" lists.

Well, as luck would have it, one year, a parent came along and made it her goal to get us new stage curtains. We fundraised and were able to purchase beautiful new stage curtains with a blue velvet one in front and black wing curtains on the sides and back. Not even three months later, the district went around taking down all of the non-fire retardant curtains, and although mine were brand spanking new with documentation, the district felt the need to remove the downright stage curtain to test. We had to do our fall show without a front right curtain (not wanting to pester them, I was patient) Six months later, right before our spring performance, lo and behold, they figured out that the curtain was fine and put it back up.

I'm not sure what the deal with curtains is in our district, because years later, there was another curtain situation.

The district decided to improve our classrooms by painting and putting in new floors and new curtains. At first, I asked them not to come in at all because I was afraid of them doing something to change my room to a way I didn't like, but the room badly needed paint and my room had a moldy carpet. The last time it had been painted was when I painted it myself in 1991 and every year my room leaked when it rained getting the carpet wet and moldy, even though, to their credit, they tried every year to fix the leak. I agreed to let them come in, and I told them as clearly as possible, the curtains are in excellent shape and do not need to be replaced. I had taken great care of the curtains in my room, so I told everyone I could to please leave them alone.

When I got back to school in the fall, you guessed it, they messed with the curtains. They took down all but one panel of curtains because I came in and stopped them from taking down more. I went to the dumpster to fish my curtains out, but the dumpster had been emptied. They did not put up new curtains since they did not order them for my classroom since I told them they were fine and didn't need to be replaced!

This time I decided not to be patient. I knew that if I didn't bug the facilities department, it would be all year before I had curtains.

I started by talking to my principal and our custodian, and then I emailed the head of facilities every single week, sometimes twice in one week. I told him how I had asked them not to remove my curtains, I told him how difficult it was to use the overhead projector when I couldn't darken the room. Then I came up with the best reason of all: I told him that if we ever had a hostile intruder on campus and had a lockdown, my students would not be safe. That finally did the trick.

I do not like to bug people. I'm sure if the head of facilities happens to run into me in town now, he will not be happy to see me. What was my choice? I have known teachers who have dealt with horrible working conditions in their classrooms the entire year or more, and nothing is done to get it rectified. For example, the district took down the stage curtains at the high school the same year they took down mine (about 15 years ago), and finally last year a parent took it upon herself to write a grant for stage curtains. Up until then they had black panels which looked like sheets hung up. I didn't understand how black panels were considered fire retardant.

Some things I had taken into my own hands when I could. For example, I also had side curtains (curtains!!) off the stage where there used to be doors. They were taken down for emergency exits and nothing from the district was put in their place. We put up thick black curtains and no one said anything for years.

For some reason, the district decided to focus on those black stage curtains in the doorways and told us to take them down. After removing them, everyone was able to see back stage, which was a problem for our performances.

My principal tried to get the curtains fire-proofed, but she only had so much time, so I decided to make it my mission to deal with the curtains. I called the fire extinguisher person, met with him, arranged everything, and got it done. It still took me six months. If I had waited for facilities to do it, the stage would still not have those side curtains. I do understand the facilities department is extremely busy and serves a lot of people. There were many things I lived with knowing they had better things to do; however, there were also things, like a front stage curtain, I could not do without.

My advice to you is this. Unless, as I said, you have a district waiting around to serve you, you need to be incredibly pro-active with anything you need in your classroom or working area. You cannot put in a work order and wait around thinking someone is going to magically appear and fix your problem. If you can fix it, and are allowed to fix it, do it.

If it is something the district HAS to do, and something you absolutely need to do your job, give them a chance to do it. If they don't do it in a timely fashion, start to pester them. Will you be popular? Unfortunately, no. Let's face it, you have to be in your work environment every day and you have to be able to function effectively. I couldn't do a spring performance with the downright stage curtain missing. I couldn't use the overhead projector for a lesson in my classroom with no curtains. These were basic necessities. If you have a similar situation, don't sit back and wait. Always be respectful, but advocate for yourself. The facilities department is busy, but so are you.

The Most Scary Haunted House of All: Angry Moms!

If you're like most teachers, you hate to call parents. I mean, you really hate it, and you will do most anything so it doesn't get to the point where you have to call a student's home. We had a discipline policy where, if after several warnings, you could send the student to a detention room. BUT, and this is a big huge BUT, if you sent the student there, you HAD to call home. Many teachers avoided using the detention room, even though they would LOVE to send the kid to it. They just did not want to have to call the student's home.

Why do teachers not want to call home? It's simple really, you never know what you're going to get when you do. You can attempt to get some information before putting yourself in that position. You ask around to the other teachers, "Have you ever called so and so's parents?" If the answer is, "Yes, I have, and the parents yelled at me and said it was my fault," then you can forget anyone else calling them.

If the answer is, "Yes, I called and they said the right things, but nothing has changed," then you may figure it won't hurt to call. At least then you can send the student to the detention room, you can document the incident and the phone call, and you won't get yelled at.

Of course, the best case scenario is when you hear, "Yes, I called the house and the parents are supportive! I saw a difference in the student's behavior after I called home." Those are the students you generally don't have to call home for often because the parents are actually parenting. They are supportive of the school and the teachers, and they also support their child. They will listen to what you have to say before automatically believing their kid. If a parent has a child in the class of a teacher who isn't the best fit, they will either tell their kid, "In life you have to deal with all kinds of people. You'll be fine." Or they will quietly find a way to transfer their child to another class without causing a lot of drama.

But now back to the scary phone calls.

I used to say to myself, "Vickie, if you can get through this day and not get a call from a parent and not have to call a parent, it's a good day!" Teachers are masters at getting close to the "have to call the parent" line. Sometimes we lose control, we say something we regret, we cringe, and we think, "WHY, OH WHY, DID I SAY WHAT I DID TO UPSET THE STUDENT??? Now I'll worry all day or night or weekend I'm going to see the dreaded message in my email the parent of so and so called!!" Sometimes you can smooth it over with the student before it's too late. You can say, "I'm sorry. I know you're a great kid," or "doing a great job," or whatever to keep them from going home and telling their parents what you said!

Sometimes you will sweat it out for 24 hours and then get lucky and you won't get a call. Whew! You think to yourself, "I'm not going to get myself in that position again." Lo and behold, it may happen again because, let's face it, we're human beings with emotions...not robots!

The worst, and I mean absolute worst, is when you get an angry mother. As the title of this chapter states there's not too many things for a teacher scarier than an angry mom. I used to tell teachers a room full of angry moms would be the most frightening haunted house anyone could imagine.

To be fair, and as a mother myself, I know how it is to be a Mama Bear protecting her cub. It's a very powerful instinct. Also, the mother being called may be dealing with many struggles in her life. She may be a single mom, working two jobs, or simply upset because she loves her child and is feeling frustrated, or even a little guilty about how her child is performing in school. She may actually believe you are picking on her child, even though most teachers don't have the time or energy to single out a student to pick on. The most important thing to remember when calling a mother is to be kind and calm.

In my 33 years of teaching, I had maybe a handful of angry dads. I could count them on one hand. Usually the dads were pretty reasonable and realistic about their kids. They would often listen to what I had to say, and then look at their kid and ask, "What do you have to say for yourself? Why do you think you have the right to disrupt this woman's class?" Or something along those lines. On the outside, I had a look of concern, but on the inside, I was so relieved the father was holding his child accountable.

Moms, unfortunately, are generally a different story. I have had supportive moms, but you have to be SO careful with moms. You can't tell it like it is with the student's misbehavior as you can when you talk to the dads. You have to start out with a SUPER concerned voice as if you are just SO worried about their child. When you mention he or she is doing nothing and failing your class, you have to behave like it breaks your heart, even though in reality you have done everything except pick up the pencil and do the work for them yourself.

When you are telling the mom about how the child is disrupting your class every single day, you can't have an ounce of frustration in your voice. You have to be smooth as honey as you tell them how concerned you are they are not getting all of the academic information because they seem distracted. Tell them it worries you because you certainly don't want to see them get behind and fail.

When I first started teaching, I made mistakes when I called parents and, boy, did I learn fast. I left a frustrated voice mail on a mom's phone, and she was not happy! The student was eating chips in class and not doing any work. He was failing and he was being disruptive. I made the mistake of calling the mom while I was feeling angry about his behavior. She called back yelling at me about how I treated her son and how he had the right to eat in class if he was hungry. I had to back-pedal big time.

Other times, moms I called were hit and miss. You called them one time, and they were totally on your side. They let you know how frustrated they were and how they didn't know what to do with their child. And then you called again, all confident they were going to support you, and they went off about how the kid said you did such and such and the mom acts like she forgot this child has been getting calls from school since they were in kindergarten.

The most important bit of advice I can give you about calling home is to call, no matter how scary it is. It's best for you, for the disruptive student, and for all of the other students in the class if you hold that student accountable. I found if I spent a lot of time at the beginning of the year calling home, then I didn't really have to as the year progressed. Word got out I called home and students didn't generally want the teacher to call their home with a negative report of their behavior. Of course, you can always make positive calls home too. Making those can ease the negative ones. Be sure when you make the calls about the student who is failing, or in trouble, you use the most concerned voice you can. If you said something you shouldn't have, apologize. Try not to get frustrated and defensive. Feel free to defend yourself, in a calm and concerned way. Approaching parents this way worked for me.

Your Dog and Pony Shows:
Aka: The Parent-Teacher Connection

There are several times in the year when you are on the frontline with the parents. First, I want to write about Back-to-School Night. I don't think I have ever met anyone who actually enjoys Back-to-School Night. Everyone is tired. It is one more thing for administrators and your School Office Supervisor to plan. Teachers have been working all day, and all they want to do is go home.

Parents have also been working all day, and the last thing they generally want to do is rush around, make dinner, figure out a babysitter for their kids (or take the kids with them), and come to school to sit and listen to their kid's teachers talk all about what they're doing in the classroom.

When I "performed" at a Back-to-School Night, (and believe me when I say it was a performance), I generally had a pretty exhausted audience. I often dreaded the whole evening, but once there, I found the parents to be pretty supportive as they looked at me with tired eyes. In fact we were all there to show we cared about the kids, and the truth is, we did care: we were just tired!

I've worked with principals who sent home a note giving information about Back-to-School Night asking parents not to bring their children since this is a night for parents. In those cases, the school would often have leadership students on campus to babysit kids whose parents needed to bring them. I loved when the principal sent out those notes. But there were also principals who not only invited, but encouraged parents to bring their children to Back-to-School Night. It was the worst!

What generally happened on those nights was the students who attended the school were restless because they had already heard all of this information. Sometimes they misbehaved, and often the exhausted parent would just sit there and not do anything about the bad behavior. By then, I would think to myself, "Am I supposed to discipline this child with their parent sitting right there?" I would go with instinct. If the parent seemed supportive of me, I might have asked the child to pay attention. If the parent seemed combative in any way, I would just keep talking until time was up. The last thing any teacher wants is to get in an altercation with a parent under any circumstances.

Every so often, one of those parents would show up who wanted everyone to know how smart they were. They would raise their hand and have a certain look on their face letting me know, "Uh, oh, it's one of THOSE parents."

The parent would say something like, "I have noticed my child is reading the novel (fill in the blank), and I'm wondering if the theme is relevant to today's political climate," or something along those lines. This parent just wanted to show off and wasn't really interested in the answer to his or her question. I did my best to answer and then allowed the person to ramble on a bit displaying their vast understanding of literature while the other parents looked at me sympathetically. Those types of parents only showed every few years, and it actually become rather amusing to watch and listen to them trying to prove how smart they were.

As I said earlier, most parents were weary, and nodded, and smiled while I rattled off my "spiel." I truly appreciated their non-verbal support.

I'm writing about Back-to-School Night because many new teachers can get rattled looking out at a sea of parents.

This is what I would tell any teacher who asked about Back-to-School Night

Dress appropriately. Parents, same as the students, make a judgment about you before you open your mouth. You will have better luck gaining their confidence if you dress and behave like the professional you are.

Carry yourself with confidence. Again, just as what you are wearing, your body language speaks volumes beyond the words you say.

Greet them at the door. Ask their name, and which student is their child.

Introduce yourself. Before launching into your curriculum, make a personal connection with them.

Write out your topics to discuss. Don't try to wing it. At our school we only had to speak for ten minutes each period. It is amazing how much you can say in a short amount of time. I often felt as if my mouth was disconnected from my body the way I would ramble on about my curriculum, grading policy, homework policy, discipline policy, and any other information I felt important to impart.

No matter how tired you are, exude positive energy. Parents don't want to think their child is spending all day with a teacher who doesn't bring positive energy into the classroom. It makes it seem as if you don't care.

Thank them for coming. At my school, there were a lot of parents who didn't show up, so I really appreciated the parents who made the effort.

Remember, most parents aren't really listening to everything you're saying. Parents are there to get a "feeling" about you. Do you know what you're doing? Do you care about their kid? Do you like your job? Those are the things most parents are ascertaining (other than maybe the one parent who wants to show you how smart he or she is).

Parents are similar to the students you teach because, resembling your students, parents want to feel confident all is well in your classroom.

Thoughts on Open House:

Open House is another face-to-face contact with parents, but it is a little different story. With Open House, you don't have to stand and talk non-stop all night while weary eyes stare at you. Parents can come in and out freely. It seemed to me most people were in better spirits for Open House. By this time, you have a relationship with your students (and know their name! Unlike Back-to-School Night, whereby you have only known your students a couple of weeks, and sometimes you have to pretend to know who their child is when parents introduce themselves).

With Open House, you can put a bunch of student work all around the room for parents to look at instead of staring at you! One year, I even set up my Karaoke system. Parents and students stopped by to sing a song. Most of all, everyone is happy the end of the year is nearing and it's almost summer. Similar to Back-to-School Night, dress and behave like a professional and exude good energy. You want to end the year on a positive note.

Thoughts on Parent-Teacher-Conferences:

Parent-Teacher Conferences are another opportunity to meet with the parents. Through the years my former school did parent conferences many different ways. When I first started teaching at my school, parents would make appointments and meet in our classrooms. Later our school decided we would meet in the library with one student surrounded by all his or her teachers at a table. The last several years of my teaching, everyone met in the multi-use room with parents waiting until their child's teacher was available. During a few years in the multi-use room, we were given an egg timer and we were instructed to move the parents along when it dinged. I never felt right rushing parents and didn't. Occasionally, however, the counselor would come by and gently remind me to wrap it up because another parent was waiting.

Personally, I preferred the idea of parents meeting in my classroom. It was private and gave parents more of a safe environment to share personal information with me if they desired.

Parent conferences are important for many reasons. I used to think the main reason for the conferences was for me to tell the parents how their child was doing. It's important for a teacher to share with the parent whatever information possible about the child. However, after thinking more deeply about it, I realized the parent conference was mostly important for the parent to share information about their child with me. Sensitive information is best shared in a quiet and private setting. Not in the noisy multi-use room filled with teachers, parents, students, and possibly an egg timer.

Parents, even in the noisy setting of the multi-use room, would often share information which would help me to better understand their child. Some conferences would be light and lively, while others would break my heart. Some parents with A+ students would simply want to hear how amazing their child was. I was okay with the egg timer going off on those. Don't get me wrong, I appreciated the A+ students, still there were only so many superlatives a teacher can summon when put on the spot.

Whether the child was struggling or superlative, I came to realize it meant a lot to the students that their parent cared enough to come to the conference and meet his or her teachers.

It could be frustrating when I would meet with a parent, talk about the child's grades, the upcoming projects, strengths and weaknesses of the child, and what to do to improve (if appropriate), only to see no change take place with the student. But even if the child did not change, my perception of the child changed. I saw a bigger picture of the child, which included his or her family and home life. The conference helped me to better serve the student.

I always appreciated the parents who showed up for their kids. It could be easy to forget how young my students were until I saw them next to mom or dad. Even when parents wouldn't make it to the conferences for various reasons, I was reminded of the fact most parents loved their children and were entrusting me to care for them and their education. As exhausting as it could be to do conferences after teaching all day, it was truly a valuable connection.

Staff Meetings: A Necessary Evil or a Complete
Waste of Time?

When I first started teaching, we only had staff meetings once a month. They were held in the morning; we were expected to be there at 8:00, and since school started at 8:45, the longest they could keep us was 8:40. Some people would take advantage of this fact, and run in at 8:05, 8:10, or, heaven forbid, as late as 8:15. Soon the district wised up and started having the staff meetings after school.

The bell schedule would vary from year to year, and, I suppose, not surprisingly, the bell schedule was often dictated by the bus schedule. In our district, the buses had to pick up and drop off the high school students first, then the elementary, and last was the middle school. Unless we wanted high school kids to be at to school by 6:00 in the morning, we had to be patient in getting our students to school. The beginning of the day dictated the end of the day. My last year teaching, the students were released at 3:45 and our staff meetings would begin promptly at

4:00. It would be announced over the loud speaker the meeting was commencing, and all kinds of tools were used to get us there by 4:00. You had to sign in, one principal gave raffle tickets to those who were on time, and sometimes glares to those who were not.

I was okay with the once-a-month meeting. I even liked them sometimes because we would get to see other teachers we may not see during the work day. Depending on the principal, we may have fun joking around with each other. Once we even had a "Slip, Trip, and Fall" video made by teachers showing all the ways we could injure ourselves at school if we weren't being careful. It was hilarious! The meetings often bonded the staff.

All that changed a few years ago.

Meetings started to get a lot more serious. About five years ago, it was decided by someone we needed a once a month staff meeting and a once a month Professional Development meeting (also known as a PD). It was also decided that we needed a weekly Professional Learning Community (PLC). I felt this was overkill. I couldn't do much about the PLC because the kids were released early so the PLCs could take place. I really hated the twice a month meetings, especially since I ran an afterschool drama program and couldn't rehearse those days. I went to our Union Rep to see if they could keep us until 5:00 twice a month and I found out they could. I figured out a way to work around it with assistant coaches. If I had to attend a meeting after school, one of my coaches would run rehearsal that day.

Then, my last year, the principal decided we needed to meet every week, and again, I was told there was nothing in our contract to prevent her from keeping us after school that often.

Meetings can be killers. Half the time they don't have anything to do with the subject you are teaching. It is a box your administrator has to check off, and it doesn't matter if the information is helpful to you or not. Many of us felt so depressed after a meeting we didn't know if we even wanted to be teachers anymore.

It's interesting because, if everyone respected the principal, they would listen attentively, even if they were dying inside. BUT if the principal was not respected, people would be checking their phones, grading papers, or having side conversations. I found teachers to be like our students, meaning if the person in charge didn't command our respect and attention, we would only pretend to listen.

One of the things I really disliked at meetings was when administrators would put up those gigantic post-it notes and give us markers and ask us to go around and write on them. They would have one they would call the "parking lot" which was where you put all of your concerns not addressed at the meeting. They said they would get back to you on those. I never recall anyone ever getting back to me about my sticky note on the parking lot.

My advice to you is to not take the staff meetings or PDs too seriously. Be respectful at the meetings, try to focus, and attempt to take everything with a grain of salt. Don't allow the meetings to discourage you about teaching.

For example, we had a vice principal who called us "Leaders of Learning," which rubbed most teachers the wrong way. At staff meetings he gave us a notebook and told us to do "Mirror Writing." He would give us some sort of esoteric prompt, but instead of writing on the given prompt, I would write out my frustrations about the meeting and how I would rather be at rehearsal with my drama students. Fortunately, reading our entries aloud was always on a volunteer basis, which I made sure of before I wrote out how I felt. Doing my writing helped me a whole lot more than writing about whatever nonsense was assigned.

Another principal expected us to have all sorts of specific methodology every period, and she wanted to be able to pop by at any point in your lesson and see one of the steps. We were instructed to write on the white board in our classrooms a very specific objective for the day's teaching. The objective needed to include a learning and language piece. Also, before students left the class at the end of the period, we needed to do a "checking for understanding" activity. It was a lot to ask us to do this six periods a day, every single day. We were supposed to have it all on the board in advance so when she "popped in" she could see all our thinking. If she came by after we had finished a step, we were told to stop whatever we were doing and do it again so she could check it off for data. Never mind the fact sometimes lessons take longer than one period to explain to students and also there are a million different variables that could happen in your classroom with 30+ middle school students.

I noticed our administrators weren't able to accomplish the objective/checking for understanding they wrote for the meetings even once or twice a month with teachers. Yet, they expected us to do it six times every day with students! In the plan they wrote out for us for the meeting, we teachers were often confused about what was expected of us, and generally it would be 5:00 p.m. and people were leaving without any sort of "checking for understanding." When I confronted my principal about my observation, she responded with, "I'm not saying I can do it either." What?

When I realized they were just checking some sort of box, I began to relax and not worry about the meetings. They generally would not follow through on something they said they were going to do. Something which would scare us, for instance, when they said they were going to drop by every classroom once a week. They couldn't follow through on such a time-consuming idea. They would do it, MAYBE once, and then a fight between students would break out, or they would have to be at the district office, or some other situation took their time and attention, and we rarely saw them.

Some principals would allow me to have drama rehearsals and get staff meeting notes from another teacher. I really appreciated those principals. Some principals demanded I be at these meetings, and I would have to figure out an alternate solution. No matter what, I realized, until something actually happens, don't worry about it. Focus on the kids and what you're doing in your classroom, and don't get too worried about what is said in the meetings. Nod your head and go back to your classroom, shut the door, and teach.

You Can't Fight City Hall - But you can try!

As the old saying goes, you can't generally fight the powers that be. It's often the case with teaching. You want to do fun things for the students and it seems you're frequently told no.

I've never been an administrator, and I imagine if I had ever walked a mile in their moccasins, I might have a better understanding of why they might say no to something I thought would be fun. However, I was never been one to take no for an answer, and neither should you.

Now, sometimes, I had no choice but to accept no. If I really wanted to do something, however, I would put up a fight before giving up. Often there was another way to make it happen, and if there was, I would find it. My fear about new teachers, and this is one of the reasons for writing this book, is they won't realize, as the saying goes, "When one door closes, look for a window." I even told administrators to find a way to say yes to new teachers because if they hear enough no's, they may simply give up. I was always on the lookout for those open windows and wouldn't give up.

Being a drama teacher, I was constantly working with the business office and my Associated Student Body account (ASB). To get money out of my ASB account seemed like an act of God. It was even complicated to put the money into the account. I understood the district wanted to make sure the money was not being embezzled. Awareness didn't make accepting the process any easier.

New teachers are often not told much. They can be in the dark about a lot of things until they are slammed against the wall. For example, when trying to run a club, fundraise, go on a field trip, or anything else that requires spending money on students, they may be caught completely off guard. Suddenly they are handed a pile of paperwork to fill out, told about the chain of bureaucracy their request would have to go through, and given deadlines to get everything done.

Sometimes, by the time the teacher figures out what they want to do, it is too late for them to do it. I would start all paperwork for my drama club activities and November fundraiser the day I got to school in August. Unless someone thinks to tell this to a first year teacher, they have no idea what they will be up against if they want to do anything extra-curricular involving money.

You can't fight city hall when it comes to the ASB. There are strict guidelines, and the business office has to go through audits, so there is no way they're going to allow you to bend the rules. However, one way to get around the red tape is to go through your Parent Teacher Association (PTA) if you can and if you are fortunate enough to have one.

For years my drama classes did a fundraiser selling singing telegrams. It involved student groups choreographing a portion of a song to sell; they would be delivered the day before spring break. The drama students would sell each telegram for $1.00. Once we were finished selling them, I would deposit the money into my ASB account to use for our yearly drama needs. This went on for years. My last year, the new principal told me I had to do ASB paperwork to even sell the telegrams. In order to do a fundraiser through ASB, I had to have a meeting with my drama club, then submit meeting notes to a Student Council meeting, which was only held once a month. Once approved by the Student Council, the request would travel downtown with additional paperwork for another approval. This process could take, at the minimum 30-45 days. I did not have a month to do this for singing telegrams! I was planning to start selling them in a few days and deliver them in two weeks. So I came up with a solution.

At times, I had used the strategy, "Do it and apologize later." I had always been one to stay under the radar, going about my business with the desire to be left alone to do my job. When it came to fundraising, the "being left alone" strategy simply did not work. I had to find a way to work around it and fast. There was no way I was going to disappoint my students and tell them we couldn't do singing telegrams because of new information I was JUST TOLD. Singing Telegrams had been a tradition at my school the day before spring break for 27 years! Not to mention it would be my last year doing them since I was retiring in June.

My solution? The PTA! With the PTA, you do not have to do all of the paperwork required with ASB. True, there is some bureaucracy involved, but it is bureaucracy "light" versus the business office which is the whole nine yards and then some!

I went to the president of the PTA and asked if I could run my singing telegram fundraiser through them. She agreed. I was relieved.

Many other situations would not work with the PTA. For example, as I stated earlier, if you want to do a field trip, run a club, or other actions that require district approval there is paperwork required that must be run through the business office.

My advice is this: if you want to fundraise, or go on a field trip, or purchase something for your classroom with your club money, find out what is required BEFORE you need whatever it is. Plan far ahead. I have seen so many teachers think they could do something, tell the students and get them all excited, only to be told "NO! You can't do it."

The teachers become discouraged and frustrated because they want to do something exciting for kids. They are willing to give of themselves and their time, yet the administrator is putting the "kibosh" on it. I have to believe there are reasons administrators say no. It most likely has something to do with a potential lawsuit, probably about inequity for students, or possibly a state or district rule. Find out what the problem is and see if there is a way to work around it. Don't give up!

Taking over Another Teacher's Assignment Mid-Year

I f you are an unemployed teacher, and you get a job taking over for another teacher mid-year, I have two words for you: Good Luck! It is one of the most difficult teaching jobs you can possibly have. It's hard to succeed because if the students loved the teacher, they will resent you and blame you for their beloved teacher no longer being there, even though, of course, it is not in any way your fault.

If the students didn't like the teacher, they have already become sort of a "gang" against the teacher; when you come in you are an outsider and another person for them to dislike. Not to mention you are walking into a classroom possibly set up in a way that doesn't work for you. If you try to change the rules so late in the year, you could have a mutiny on your hands.

The time when I have seen this work the best is when people do a job share, and it is arranged ahead of time. Two teachers are hired for one position and they divide it into two parts. They may split the days of the week in two or they may split the year, whereby one teacher teaches the fall semester and the other teacher teaches the spring semester. This way the students know both teachers who work together to have consistency in the class-room and are sharing the same expectations. In this situation it is similar to two parents raising a family. My son was in a class using this model one year, and it worked well. He ended up liking one of the teachers better than the other, but he accepted the situa-tion since both teachers did a good job preparing the students.

Having someone new come in mid-year in an elementary classroom, may work okay. When I was a child in 4th grade, our teacher was quite old and became ill. We got a long term sub (although I had no idea at the time that's what she was, I only knew we had a different teacher now). Then another teacher came in and I moved to a new classroom with her and some of my classmates. As a young student, I rolled with all of the changes with the three teachers with no problem. I realize not everyone can.

It was a different story when I taught at the high school. I had just graduated from college and was subbing in the spring until school started in the fall. I got a sub job for the day at the high school for a beloved teacher who was out on mater-nity leave. The students had had a different substitute teacher every day. I had never experienced anything like that classroom and college certainly did not prepare me for what I faced. The students were beyond angry their sweet teacher had abandoned them. There was nothing I could do to calm them down. They were out of control, throwing things across the room and had no intention of behaving. Two of the students pulled me aside and explained what was going on in the room and sort of looked after me. Still it was horrible.

I finally called the administration in to remove some of the kids. I suspect it hurt my chances to work at that school since the principal may have believed I didn't have good classroom management. No one could have controlled those students! I was fortunate that it was only for a day and not a long term sub position. The irony was one of the worst kids ended up being in my summer school class at a different high school. (I encourage you to teach summer school while trying to get a permanent teaching position). He was shocked to see I would now be his teacher! Fortunately, he did not give me an ounce of trouble all summer.

At my school, I saw this situation more times than I can count. A teacher leaves for some reason, and a long term sub comes in. The students have already bonded as a group and in comes the outsider. The class makes this poor teacher's life miserable. I saw kids take bets on how long it would take to drive out the sub. I saw the principal defend the kids and not the sub because the principal is so afraid of getting flak from the parents. One teacher was so shaken from being treated horribly by the students when she was in a long term sub position she was afraid to go back into the classroom for ten years.

In the students' defense, I don't always blame them for feeling upset. They feel cheated and abandoned when they have bonded with a teacher and the teacher decides to leave. One teacher at our school quit after the first day because he got a job for a better paying position at a neighboring school district, and those kids had one long term sub after another all year. They lost a year of math and were behind the other students who had a stable math teacher. It affected our entire campus.

Once in a blue moon a long term sub works out and becomes a permanent teacher. If a long term sub can pull together a class dealing with teacher abandonment and succeed, the teacher is a treasure. He or she has walked the hot coals and has come out alive, and will make an amazing permanent teacher. Although it's rare, I have seen it happen.

Basically, I'm saying, know what you are getting yourself into if you choose to come in mid-year and ask as many questions as you can think to ask. Visit the classroom and, if possible, speak with the teacher who is leaving. Walk around the campus to get a feel of the school, ask about the discipline policy, and try to get a sense of the principal's support for teachers. You are probably going to experience initiation under fire and, if you succeed, it could lead to a full time job and a better life next year when you have your own classroom and a group of students who bond to you.

It is understandable you may be tempted to accept the position because you need the money, or believe it will give you the opportunity to be known in a district and get your foot in the door for a permanent position. Considering my tips can prepare you for what to expect. You have to decide if you are up for that challenge and proceed accordingly and with caution. However, if you are taking over an unruly class and cannot settle them down, as I said previously, you may be seen as a person with poor classroom management skills. Perception is important, and being seen in a negative light may make it difficult for you to get another position.

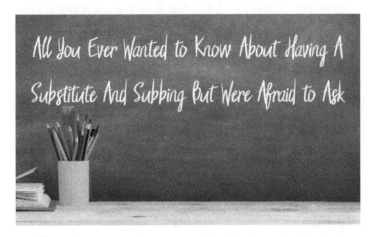

All You Ever Wanted to Know About Having A Substitute And Subbing But Were Afraid to Ask

O kay, so maybe you weren't afraid to ask. Maybe you didn't know what questions to ask. This chapter is about tips for when you need to have a sub. It's also tips, for if and when, the school asks you to sub for another teacher on your prep period. It's a call you may dread.

First of all, substitute teaching is a hard gig. If you are reading this and are not yet a credentialed teacher, but you have gotten your bachelor's degree and are subbing, let me assure you that subbing is NOTHING like actually teaching. Before I got my permanent teaching job, I was a substitute teacher. I would go into different schools where I didn't know anyone and be possibly treated like a pariah in the staff lounge (see chapter about the staff lounge). The students loved to test me, which was exhausting every period. Sometimes I would walk into a hornet's nest, while other times it would be a great day.

I got so disillusioned with subbing I went back to work in a bank until the fall when I started a fulltime teaching job. Because of what I went through, I was always strict with how my students treated the sub the rare time I was absent. I hated to be absent because I had to do a lot of work to set things up for the sub. Then usually I had to clean up a mess upon my return.

Here are some things you can do to make a sub day go as successfully as possible:

Do your best to get a good sub in your classroom. If at all possible, do all you can to get a reliable person in your room while you're absent. The best way to do that is to have a good reputation for classroom control and for leaving good instructions for the sub. If someone subs for you, and their day is a nightmare, no one but the worst sub who can't get a job anywhere else, will come back for you. If you're lucky to get anyone!

Write Down all of your classroom expectations. If you want things to go smoothly, write down all of your rules for the sub. Write down your policies on cell phones, hats, changing seats, bathroom passes, gum, eating, and everything else that is in your classroom management plan. Students will say whatever to get what they want, so the sub needs to know the truth. You only need to write this once, but make sure to include it in every sub plan packet.

Don't expect the sub to do the lesson you can do: Make the lesson plan super user-friendly. Don't think that a complete stranger can come in and do some complicated lesson plan. Yes, it's true, you will probably lose a day of instruction while you're out. Accept it. Still, DO leave a lesson plan!

Lock up all valuables: I was often surprised at the choices kids made when their regular teacher wasn't there. When I knew I would be absent, I would tell the kids, "I'm not dead. You will see me again. Make good choices while I'm out, and if you see other kids making bad choices, don't join in; stay under the radar and stay out of trouble!" Sometimes they would do things with a sub they would never dream of doing with me. When I was absent, I locked up all of my dry erase markers (except one), my teacher's edition of the textbook, and my remote control for the projector (unless the sub needed these items, in which case I would put them in a special place and tell the sub where to find them). Also I would lock up anything personal I was concerned students may want to have. I put away anything that would tempt students. I didn't want to give students any ammo to get themselves into trouble.

Whatever you threaten to do if the kids misbehave while you're out, DO IT when you return: True, it is a pain to be out. You have to do all of this prep, and you HOPE that you will get a good report when you return. Perhaps you promised a reward for good behavior with the sub. Great, do it if the students succeed. That's easy to do. The hard thing is when you said a threat about any bad behavior with the sub, "If you do this, I will do that." And, then you get back, and there's a list with a few names of kids who tested the sub (Arrgghhh!). Whatever it was you said you would do, you HAVE to do, so be careful what you say. If you don't do it, you can forget your word meaning anything next time, and chances are there will be a next time!

Don't have the sub collect ANY work or anything from the kids: When I was absent, I told the students to not give anything to the sub. The reason? When I first started teaching, I would return, and when I went through the stack of papers, I would notice certain students' work was missing. And what would the students say? You guessed it: "I gave it to the sub!" Now it's your word against theirs. Good luck if their parents call. I would make sure to tell the students, I would write the information for the sub in my notes, and I would write it on the board: Do not give anything to the sub!

What if the school calls you to sub on your prep period? If your school is short on substitutes like ours, then you may be called to cover a class on your prep period. At our school we had the right to say no. You would get paid for this service, yet I did not like giving up my time this way. However, every so often, I would agree to do it because I was fond of the School Officer Supervisor or a teacher friend would ask me. Your school may not ask this of you. Your school may require you to do it. The following are a few ways I was able to cope when having to cover for another teacher on my prep period.

Tips if you are asked to sub for another teacher on your prep period:

Bring students to your own classroom: Generally, if they are asking you to give up your prep period, they are grateful if you say yes because it means the administrators don't have to do it. They are not going to be choosy about how you cover the class. I have found when students are on my turf, they don't feel as powerful as when you're coming into their world. When they're in your room, you get to decide where they sit, which also breaks down their power as a group. If you are subbing for what you know is a very sweet class, you may not choose to do this, but if there is ANY doubt about the students, bring them to your room instead of going to theirs.

Take care of yourself with the lesson plan: If you get some complicated lesson plan from the teacher, don't worry about doing it. I am not a math teacher, so if I had to sub math, I would either choose a student I knew to run the lesson while I managed the class, or I could say forget it and showed a movie. What you don't want to do is drive yourself crazy trying to figure out some lesson plan while the kids are getting restless, bored, and out of control.

Remember, you will have to teach your own students the rest of the day and your allegiance is to them. Yes, you want to be a good soldier and help the other teachers, but I found most teachers are just so happy you subbed for them they are not angry you didn't cover their lesson on trigonometry. Also, if they aren't happy with the job you did, maybe they'll be better prepared and get an actual substitute or call on another teacher next time.

As I said before, subbing is a hard job. People who are good subs are golden and you want to do everything in your power to help them succeed so they will want to return to be your sub. Don't be too golden subbing on your prep period because, unless you really need the extra money, one extra period could burn you out, and that's not good for you, your students, or anyone!

I n the teaching world, we have to deal with budget cuts more often than I can enumerate. One of the reasons staff meetings can be such downers is because you have to hear about the latest budget cuts coming. Everyone gets super upset. Teachers will comment, "What more can they take from us? There's no more meat on the bone!" Somehow the budget cuts come and life still goes on.

The biggest scare is when we're told teachers could lose their jobs. My first encounter was in 1990 when I was teaching on a military base. It was decided the base was closing and several of our schools would be closing too. This base closure was far-reaching in our entire district because of the students we would lose and because our district received a lot of funding from the military. Everyone was in a panic.

The district put together a list of all teachers in our district. You had a number on the list depending on your years of teaching, the need for what you taught, and your education level. Tenure did not make you safe. We were all scared! Everyone was constantly talking about the list at every morning break, meeting, and lunch break.

The conversations would go something like this:

Teacher One: "So, what number are you on the list?"

Teacher Two: "I'm number 375. I think I may be safe because I also coach football."

One: "I don't know. I hear they may not have a football team anymore. I'm probably okay because I'm number 150. I teach Special Ed."

Two: "If they don't have football at this school anymore, I don't even want to teach, and with fewer kids, they're not going to need as many Special Ed teachers."

One: "Well, I'm sure I can find a teaching job somewhere else, but I don't want to move my family."

You get the idea.

These conversations went on for months and no one really knew if they were going to survive the cut or not. Many teachers jumped ship and took a job somewhere else. I personally got lucky because I happened to be performing in a talent show to raise money for the high school baseball program. The principal at a middle school across town, not closing, asked if I wanted to come teach drama at his school. I jumped at the chance. I ended up being at the same school for 27 years until I retired. I probably would have stayed at the first school if it hadn't been in danger of being closed.

It was strange the year the school was going to close because people were coming from other schools and taking books, furniture, and other items right out of our classrooms while we were still teaching there. I felt like Ebenezer Scrooge in "A Christmas Carol" when they were robbing his home as he watched.

In the end, the school never closed. Even though they closed the base, the military homes became available to civilians, and many families moved in. At first, the district didn't know what to expect, so they renamed Fitch Middle School to Lower Marshall and the elementary nearby to Upper Marshall.

When they realized there were lots of kids, they named it back to Fitch Middle School. Today it's called Seaside Middle. It never closed, not even for a minute. The district scrambled to fill the teaching positions of all the teachers who jumped ship. Needless to say, it took years to stabilize the mess that was made.

A few years later, more budget cuts, and more teacher layoffs. Although I had tenure, I was given a pink slip, and I have to say it did not feel good. Remembering what happened in 1990, I didn't panic or leave or do anything at all. I kept teaching, and, sure enough, my pink slip was rescinded and the district frantically tried to rehire everyone who had left and fill the positions of those who went to other districts.

The drama department had been on the chopping block more often than I can recall. In the beginning, I fought for it tooth and nail and always won. Once my program was established and considered successful, it wasn't on the chopping block anymore.

My last year, we had the doom and gloom meeting of more budget cuts. We were told five million dollars had to be cut from our district budget. Five million dollars from a district already down to bone marrow! Our art teacher was in tears convinced her position would be cut. I pulled her aside and told her the truth. I let her know there is a very good chance her program would not be cut. Our school was going in the direction of another instructional model whereby students are required to have many elective choices. I also told her about all of the times my drama program seemed in danger only to never skip a beat. I let her know she shouldn't worry about it because she can't control what's going to happen and it most likely will not happen. If it does, I said, she would figure it out and, if necessary, find another job because she is a great teacher and there is constantly a teacher shortage.

No one told her her art class was specifically on the chopping block. If it were the case, I may have suggested she fight as I did for drama, however with the new direction the school was headed in with a focus on the arts, I didn't think they would eliminate her program. She did not get cut.

One of the solutions our district came up with was to buy out the older, more expensive teachers, like me, and keep the newer less expensive teachers, like the young art teacher. I was planning on working one more year and wasn't going to take the buyout, but the more I thought about it, the more I realized I needed to step aside while I still loved teaching and let the younger teachers have their chance.

Surviving Changes That Are Supposed to 'Fix' Everything

You're going along just fine, feeling solid in your teaching, and, wham! You are told everything is going to change. Actually what you're told is, "It's what you're already doing with a few changes." You know darn well it's going to be much more. If it truly was what you're already doing, why are you having a ton of meetings and trainings for it? I'll tell you why. You already know the truth: It isn't like what you're already doing. The only thing the same is the subject! I went through this more times than I can count.

One of the things constantly changing in our district was the bell schedule. I have taught with a six period day, a seven period day, an eight period day, a block schedule, an A Day-B Day schedule, and a rotation schedule (whereby you start with first period one day, second period the next, and so on). Within each of the 6, 7, or 8 period days, the amount of time per period varied greatly from year to year and principal to principal. When

I first started teaching, I taught for 270 minutes with 5 minute passing periods, a 45 minute lunch, and a 20 minute break. As life went on, the teaching day became 305 teaching minutes, four minute passing periods, a 30 minute lunch, and a 10 minute break. I felt as if I couldn't catch my breath or even go to the bathroom between classes. Teachers and students were becoming more stressed. We were told more time in the classroom meant "Every Moment Counts." Yes, every moment may count, but if you don't consider the basic human needs of people, everyone becomes stressed and ineffective. Personally, I always believed the administration wanted kids in the classrooms as much as possible so they wouldn't have to do so much hall duty. I can't say I blame them for feeling that way.

The bell schedule is often the first place where the district looks to fix things. My advice to you is if you have any say at all in the schedule, speak up. Your life will be extremely affected by the bell schedule. If you feel you don't have time to run to the bathroom, or speak for a minute with a student after class, you can't possibly do your best when the next 30+ students come into your room. One of the neighboring districts fought to have a maximum amount of teaching minutes written into their teaching contract. I had no idea we were not protected with a maximum amount of teaching minutes in our district contract until it was too late. I have fought and won for certain bell schedules. There were times I lost the battle. I always voiced my opinion, and I advise you to do the same.

Besides the often changing bell schedule, I lived through my share of new teaching strategies meant to fix things. I saw our district spend countless amounts of money on binders and training, only to adopt a completely new idea the next year. My former school is currently working on becoming another instructional model. I was sent to training in another state along with many other teachers, some of who also no longer work for our district. It is the latest silver bullet intended to engage students. I have nothing against the new instructional model or any new teaching strategy. I do object to more and more put on the teachers instead of expecting the students to share more in their learning. And even though the new model is student-centered instruction, there is still an enormous amount of work involved for the teachers, not to mention a huge learning curve for them.

This is my advice when the new ideas are flung at you: Take your time incorporating them into your teaching and don't panic. For all you know, there could be different new ideas the next year.

I was fortunate in a lot of ways to teach social studies and drama. Why? First of all, for the most part, the administration didn't pay much attention to my drama class. And with any new idea, they would generally focus on math and English first. When it was decided that our district would embrace Common Core, our math teachers were pulled out of class countless teaching days for training. They had to work together to come up with pages of unit plans.

Next, English had to do the same. English teachers were pulled out for days to do unit planning. This took them countless hours to create.

At the end of the school year, the social studies department was told we were next and would be pulled out for several days the next school year. But guess what? By the next year, the district decided to throw out all of the unit plans and go to the other instructional model. It was just getting going, and then our principal left. We had a year to stabilize the school, and the following year in comes a new principal. She is working diligently to implement the new program.

Please keep in mind when you are presented with a new silver bullet, it may take a while to get it going. There may not be adequate training for it, and everyone is most likely as much in the dark about what to do as you are. I wouldn't stress about it. I would also not start scurrying around trying to implement it right away because it may not even stick. Take your time, do the best you can, fold it in where it fits, and continue to do what you're already doing and know is good teaching.

How to Train Your Administrator

B efore you read this chapter, I have to offer an important caveat. What I am about to tell you is only for the tenured teacher. Unfortunately, until you have tenure, you have to be very careful. I have seen administrators let new teachers go who don't do everything they say without an argument. I actually didn't think this was possible with the teacher shortage, but I saw it happen with my own eyes a few years ago. Now I tell new teachers, "Be careful. Let the 'old salts' on the staff do the talking for you!"

An important thing to remember with an administrator is they are not God Almighty. They have a job to do same as you, and they are not your lord and master.

I had so many administrators it is hard for me to count them all. One year I had five principals! It makes me chuckle when I think of a first year teacher who was very upset because they had fired her principal, who had been very supportive of her. She didn't know what she was going to do. I told her, "Honey, get used to it and stay as autonomous as possible!"

My advice will not work if you are not doing your job. If you are an ineffective teacher who is trying to get away with doing as little as possible, you are vulnerable to scrutiny by whoever is in the administrative position. I have seen administrators do everything they can to make a tenured teacher's life miserable so they will quit or transfer to another school, and personally I completely understand their position. It isn't fair for students or the staff to endure an apathetic teacher. If you are a teacher who is burnt out, chances are you will not get along with any administrator. I suggest you stay invisible, find a different job, or hope the teachers' union protects you, which I have also seen happen many times.

For others who have a strong reputation and are doing a good job, here are some suggestions for "training" your administrator.

Introduce yourself immediately: As soon as the new principal arrives on the scene, they are going to want to know who's who. They are going to ask around about everyone on the staff. This is one of the places your solid reputation can help you. Make an appointment and have a face-to -face chat with the new administrator. Be honest about what you need to do your job. Tell the new principal about your history at the school and what you have been allowed to do in the past that was successful and you are hoping to continue doing.

For example, I had been doing chocolate bar sales for years to raise money for the drama program. I was always upfront with my new principal about it, and I was never told no. Again, I believe my good reputation helped because if I had lost money or caused problems with past sales, word on the street would have been, "Don't let her do it."

Stay out of their office and keep a low profile: Once you introduce yourself, disappear. Don't be in their office all the time bugging them. I have seen teachers who want the principal's approval about everything. Principals are sort of the Mom or Dad of the school, and some teachers feel that they need their approval for every step they take.

When you are constantly in their office or frequently emailing them, you become very visible. I always wanted to be left alone by the administration. If I needed their help, I would ask. I rarely asked. And when I did ask, they would usually help. You don't want them to think you're a pest. Do your job and let them do theirs.

Pick your Battles: I tangled with just about every principal I had, and yet there were many battles I didn't fight because I didn't want to be seen as a teacher who caused trouble. For example, when we had a ridiculous bell schedule at our school, I did research on why the bell schedule wasn't good for students or teachers, and I calmly presented my findings to my principal. She wouldn't budge. Once I did all I could, I let it go and maintained a good attitude.

One of my principals was a bully, however, and I wasn't going to stand for it. There was a room with electrical panels and we weren't allowed to store things in there; permission changed with whoever was in charge at the time. The principal at the time said I could not store props for drama in there, but my vice principal said it was fine. I came to school one morning and all of my props were thrown out of the room in disarray. I was furious. The principal got in my face about the room, and I got right back in her face letting her know that the vice principal was also my boss and said it was okay. I also told her she had no right to damage my props. We were like two cobras rising up and inflating our hoods. She ended up apologizing, and I did too. I believe we found mutual respect. She left, like so many others, after one year. I had to train another principal by telling them I knew how to do my job and I didn't need anyone breathing down my neck.

Don't think you have to say yes to everything they suggest to you: Some things you simply cannot get out of, for example, training for the new "silver bullet" or enduring an evaluation. Don't think you have to say yes to things that take extra time and are not part of your job description. For example, I was asked to be head of the social studies department. It meant extra meetings with no extra pay. I didn't care about the no extra pay, but I didn't want to commit to being department chair because it took time away from my drama rehearsals. I have known teachers who were afraid to say no, and ended up getting resentful and burnt out. One teacher said yes to the school leadership team before she found out that it entailed weekly 7:00 a.m. meetings. She was exhausted and angry about the commitment she made. She did eventually quit the team.

If nothing else, find out what you are saying yes to before agreeing. Teachers get so little praise they often jump at any recognition from "Principal Mom (or dad)" and say yes to whatever she wants and regret it later. You have the right to think about a commitment before accepting it and make sure not to say yes when you mean no!

Find things your principal is doing right: I may sound harsh, but the truth is I am quite sensitive and I do want to get along with others. I don't like conflict, although sometimes it's necessary in order for you to be able to do your job. I generally would find good in my administrators, and I would give them a small gift at the Holidays with a card saying what I appreciated about them. It was always sincere.

To me, our school was a family and, while there were struggles along the way, I always strove for harmony with my students and the staff. True harmony takes work because you have to tell the truth, which can be scary. Being authentic requires risk, and I was willing to take that risk in order to have a healthy work environment. I encourage you to be courageous and respectfully tell your truth. I think it is one of the most helpful strategies to avoid burnout.

Teacher Trust

aving teachers and staff trust you is vital to succeeding in education. It may seem obvious, still I can't tell you how many teachers I witnessed make the mistakes I will share with you. Some things in this chapter have been shared in other chapters, but like the boundaries chapter, these ideas are worth repeating because sometimes we forget basic courtesies and can get ourselves into trouble.

Like everyone, I made mistakes, and over my 33 years of teaching, I tried my best not to make the same mistake twice. One mistake I made with trust was when I was running late to my break duty, sort of on purpose. Let's just say, I was not in any great hurry to get outside to monitor hundreds of middle schoolers. I decided a good stall tactic would be to run to the ladies' room before my duty. I was in a stall and a friend came in and knew I was in there. She said, "Hey, don't you have break duty?"

"Yes, I'll get out there when I get out there," I laughed.

When I walked out of the stall, there was our counselor, and she was very disappointed in me and said, "Nice, Vickie." I was so embarrassed!! I went to her office later and apologized, and I never dragged my feet getting to break duty again. And, I NEVER had a conversation when I didn't know exactly who was in the ladies' room. My comment hurt my counselor's trust in me, and I had to fight hard to win it back. It is one example of the many lessons I learned through the "School of Hard Knocks."

Every year I sent drama students out on campus to run in and out of classrooms delivering singing telegrams. Fortunately, it was a place where I never messed up. I knew if I did not plan everything carefully, I would not have the staff's trust, and the next year when I asked to do singing telegrams, teachers would lock my kids out of their classrooms. The same is true with selling chocolate bars to raise money for drama. Selling chocolate is extremely disruptive. The kids are not supposed to sell on campus. Of course they end up doing just that! Fundraisers, in general, are very hard to navigate because learning in school has to be the top priority. But, dang it, you need the money so you have to look the other way a little when kids are all hyped up about selling. I always made it crystal clear what the rules were with selling the chocolate. I would tell my students, "If you break the rules, I won't defend you." I had to back the teachers and not the kids because, the next year, those students would be gone, but I still needed the trust of the teachers and staff to sell again. Even through a myriad of principals, I was always allowed to sell the chocolate, and I believe it was because I did my best to honor the feelings of the staff.

Here are a few other suggestions for earning and keeping trust with your co-workers:

Keep secrets. If someone tells you something, keep it to yourself. I have had situations where I told someone something and then heard it from someone else. Needless to say, I never told that person anything again.

Don't talk about other teachers to students. When students would complain to me about another teacher, I would always say, "You need to go and tell them how you feel." If the student said that they were afraid, or they tried and the teacher didn't listen, I suggested they go to the counselor or principal and, if needed, have the two of them set up a meeting with the teacher. If it was basic whining, I wouldn't listen or I would say, "Please don't talk about other teachers to me." I have known of teachers who often talk about other teachers with students, and that concerned me. It seemed they were using the students to get some need of theirs met.

Keep your students quiet in the hallways. When you are walking through the hallways with your classes on the way to the library or wherever, remember, your classroom management is on display for the entire school to see. How you walk through the hall determines your reputation. When I saw a rowdy class walk through the hall, I lost some respect for that teacher and so did everyone else, even though we didn't say it.

I would tell my students, when we walk through the hall, there is NO talking, not quiet talking since everyone has their own definition of quiet. Everyone knows what NO talking means. If they continued to talk, I would march them back to my classroom to try again. I would only have to do it once or twice a year. I can't tell you how many people commented on my quiet kids in the hallway. People notice.

Be a good neighbor: It's the same thing if you are allowing your kids outside your room to work on skits or some other project. Obviously, the NO talking rule doesn't work there. It is essential you give them directions about how loud to talk, where they can be furthest away from others' windows, and you should definitely pull students back in your classroom if they don't follow your directions. Everyone on your wing will appreciate your diligence.

Appreciate all of the support staff: Don't expect others to do things for you all the time. Remember the custodian, the School Office Supervisor, the librarian, and all other support staff have a lot of people to take care of, so when they need you to sign paperwork, or get kids to return books, or whatever, do it! Don't expect them to have to keep reminding you. If you thank them with a card or small gift, it goes a long way. If you can't, at least say thank you. The most important thing here is not to make anyone else's job harder because of you.

Don't be absent unless absolutely necessary. When you are absent, you make life challenging for everyone else. Sometimes the sub cancels, and others have to cover for you. Sometimes you have a horrible sub, and the kids are hyped up and it affects the campus and the rest of the classes. I understand people sometimes need to be absent; however, those who are absent a lot tend to lose people's trust. When I became exhausted at work, I was told, "You have so many sick days stored up. You should take a day off a month to de-stress." I had explained that taking a day off is more stress. I needed a really good reason for taking a day off.

If you do have to take a day off, follow my advice for having a substitute. Plan ahead. If not, the other teachers won't think much of you as a colleague, unless it truly was an emergency. Really, how many of those happen in an entire teaching career? Also, I don't know about private or charter schools, but if you work for the public school system, all of your sick days become part of your pay when you retire. I stored up 276 sick days, and I now get paid for those every month for the rest of my life. Consider the future with your sick days.

As I wrote in a separate chapter, use rewards sparingly. Overdoing rewards causes other teachers to wonder what the heck is going on in your classroom, and they tend to lose respect for you.

Try not to tell everyone how tired you are: I understand sometimes you need to say, "I am so tired!" What you don't want is to come off as a whiner. No one wants to constantly hear how tired you are, especially the kids. Everyone has a job to do, and, yes at times, it is exhausting! The best thing you can do is be a team player, roll up your sleeves, and do your job without a lot of complaining: Okay, maybe a little complaining. Try not to overdo it.

The main thing here is to remember your coworkers are dependent on you to keep the bigger picture of the school in mind. Yes, your job and class are important, but so is everyone else's. If you have your kids out in the hallways being loud, it's rude to all of the other classrooms. The more considerate you are of the other faculty members, the more they will be considerate of you. There will be times when you may need their help, and they will be more willing to say yes to a request if they see you as a team player and not out only for yourself.

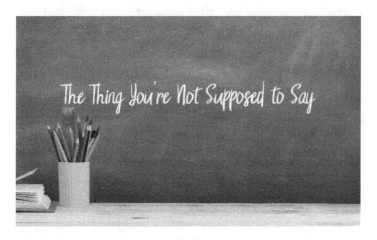

The Thing You're Not Supposed to Say

Now that I'm retired, I'm going to say it: You're not going to like every kid you teach. I know it's awful to say. I know I wouldn't want my child to be in a classroom with a teacher who did not like him; however, if a teacher didn't like my son, I would have to wonder what my son was doing in his or her class causing such a reaction. Most teachers truly want to like every student. The truth is, we're human beings with feelings. No one expects you to like every adult you work with, so how could you possibly like every student? A lot of liking someone is how the person treats you. I suppose how someone treats you is how they see you.

When I think of myself, I do not identify as a teacher. I think of myself first as a person or woman, and then a mother, or spouse, a daughter, sister, or friend. Teacher is one of my identities, and it is an important part of my life, but it is not first on my list. I was always there for my students; however, if my family needed me, they came first. Fortunately, I was seldom absent.

Everything in teaching tells you you need to connect emotionally with each and every student. And as much as I tried, there were students who made it difficult. These were students who did not treat me like a person and acted as if I was a screen who couldn't see their actions. I do have to say most students were very respectful, and I found good in almost all of my students. Every so often there was one I just could not like.

Was I respectful and polite to the student? Yes, of course. Did I wish every single day the student would be absent or transfer to another school? YES, absolutely!

So you don't think I'm horrible, let me give you one example of a student who made my life challenging. The name of the student has been changed.

There was "Dave." I tried hard to connect and find good in Dave. I would stand at my door, greeting students including Dave. If I saw him doing something good, I would be sure to point it out. I would try to have a conversation with him about something he enjoyed. I spoke with him one-on-one about his behavior. I called his parents, I met with his parents, I met with the principal and his parents, and I moved him all over the classroom to different seats. I tried everything I could think of, still it seemed all Dave wanted to do was distract everyone in my classroom from learning. I don't need to detail every distraction strategy he used. If you are a teacher, you probably have had a "Dave" in your room.

He was sent to continuation school once and then returned. The next day he was doing something illegal in class, so he was sent back to continuation only to return the following year. He quickly did something again, and it was back to continuation.

Now, you may say Dave needed love and support. You may say he probably had emotional issues preventing him from focusing or behaving, and you may be 100% right. The thing is, however, I am not a trained therapist. I did not have the privilege of working one-on-one with a child and finding out about their emotional wounds. As a history teacher, trying to teach 30+ students each period, it seemed very unfair to the other students for me to be spending a large amount of my time and energy getting Dave to behave. At one point, he was put in "Karaoke Corner," which is the place in my classroom behind my Karaoke machine. The student who sits there cannot see the other students, although they can still see me. At that point, Dave tried to distract the class by making noises. Sigh…

I admit I did not like Dave, and I was thrilled when he left my classroom, was miserable when he returned and was excited when he left again. Dave needed more help than I could possibly give him within the framework of my classroom and work day.

I am happy to say I only had one Dave every couple of years. If I had a room full of them, I never would have lasted 33 years. I'm writing about this topic because often, as teachers, we feel horrible admitting we don't like a student, and I'm telling you it is okay to feel that way. If a teacher were being completely honest, he or she would admit they too have had a Dave. I can say with almost 100% certainty any teacher who doesn't like a student has tried liking him or her, but the student has been horrible to the teacher. I have seldom known a teacher to not like a student for no apparent reason. It's generally because the student has been disruptive or disrespectful, or has refused to do any work.

If this student is destroying your classroom environment and making it almost impossible for others to learn and you would like to find a better fit for a "Dave," you will need to document how the student is not getting the educational opportunities he or she "deserves." You will need to show the educational minutes the student is losing every day. If you can prove the child is not able to learn in your classroom, you might get the student placed in a better situation for his or her learning, which would benefit everyone. What you cannot do and what will not work is focusing on how that child is distracting the other students in the class and making it difficult for them to learn. Although this never made sense to me, it is sad but true.

Keep in mind, you can only use this strategy of documenting the lost educational minutes of the disruptive student once or twice in your entire teaching career, so be sure this student warrants extreme action. If you try to do this every year, you will have no credence whatsoever. If you have a student pushing you beyond your limits, making you physically and emotionally ill, and causing you to think you should quit teaching, you may consider giving it a try.

The Firing Squad: Evaluations

Okay, so maybe it's not exactly standing in front of a firing squad, but evaluations can make you anxious, nervous, and stressed. Never having had a bad evaluation, it didn't prevent me from worrying every time I had to endure one. At our school we were evaluated every other year, and I thought it was true of all of our district schools. Later, it came as a complete surprise when discovering a friend of mine, who worked in one of our high schools across town, had never had an evaluation in the ten years she worked there. Not one to blow the whistle on anyone, I kept quiet. It certainly didn't seem fair.

Many years ago, since always having had good evaluations, a colleague told me there was a form that could be signed which excused a teacher from being evaluated for five years. I jumped at the chance to sign the form. Five years passed quickly, and I was once again up for an evaluation.

The ease of an evaluation depends so much on who is evaluating you. Having had wonderful evaluators who sat and watched me teach with positive non-verbal signs of nods and smiles, caused me to be unprepared emotionally for my last evaluation. It was the absolute worst. I had no idea at the time I would be retiring a year earlier than expected and it would be my final one.

The administrator who evaluated me was new to the job. Always being one who volunteered to go first to get my evaluation over with, it felt comfortable scheduling it early in the school year. Unfortunately, my administrator had never performed one before. It seems he was trying to really show the principal what he was made of by coming down extremely hard on me. He made a mistake in trying to make my life difficult; it's generally not a good idea to think you can push around a seasoned teacher.

He had no idea what he was doing and failed to give me the correct forms or directions. Since he hadn't given me anything, it made sense to assume the process was similar to the last time. Basically, he kept throwing additional requirements at me, and I kept back pedaling to figure out what I was supposed to be doing. He came into my class, and I was teaching up a storm, but he wasn't looking, his head was down and he was pounding away on his laptop. I passed the evaluation, but it was a miserable experience. He also got many complaints from other teachers, and he lightened up.

After that horrible experience, and never wanting to be evaluated again, I tried to sign one of those five year forms for a second time, but the district was no longer offering it. We got a new principal and vice principal the following year. My new principal was very young. She was born the year I started teaching! Since she decided to start her evaluations with first year teachers, she chose not to evaluate me.

Retiring at the end of the year, I got my wish of never having to be evaluated again.

Evaluations are hard because it feels you are being scrutinized under a microscope. Of course, it's always possible to improve and be open to positive suggestions. What is not appreciated is when the evaluator makes the teacher feel uncomfortable or afraid. An evaluation should be a positive interaction.

You never-ever want to get a bad evaluation. If the administrator doesn't feel you are competent, they will send in people to "help" you and your life becomes a living hell. No one wants someone in their classroom watching them all the time. However, it may be enough to do what you do and not stress about it. Believe you're doing a good job and don't worry about being evaluated.

My advice to you regarding being evaluated is to relax. If you have the choice of who evaluates you, ask for a person who makes you feel supported. Find out what forms are needed and ask how you are expected to fill them out. If you are required to sit down with the evaluator ahead of time, tell them what you would like from them while they are in your room. For example, I should have requested, for the person who sat and looked at his laptop, to give me non-verbal support.

Bottom line: the evaluation is supposed to help you and not hurt you. We all have things to learn and everyone can improve, but it's difficult to improve if you feel you are being criticized. Administrators are supposed to support and encourage you. We are often told to give three positive statements to students for every negative one, yet teachers are sometimes not treated with the same respect. Speak up for yourself at evaluation time and communicate what you need in order to make it a positive learning experience for you.

I have written a lot in this book about the pitfalls of teaching, but before I am finished, I also want to write about the rewards of teaching. College students often think when they become a teacher they will inspire students and change the world. In the beginning of the book, I wrote about how the reality of that belief can be like a jump into cold water when you first start teaching. The thing is, those rewards really do exist!

There were times when I got so fed up with teaching I didn't know how I was going to finish the year. Once when my family and I were sitting at dinner, and I was talking about my teaching day, my son said, "Mom, you look miserable! You need to find another job!" I wondered if he was right and I should go back to work in a bank. But every single time, and I mean every single time, I was ready to throw in the towel, something would happen to let me know I was on the right track being a teacher.

I would get a letter in my box, an email, or a visit from a former student telling me what I meant to them. I would get a gift on my desk, a hug, a letter, or card from a current student. Maybe a student would simply come up to me and tell me they loved being in my class and were looking forward to it all day. Something would happen, and I would nod my head and think to myself, "Okay, I'm going to hang in there and stick with teaching."

I have a binder full of those cards and notes from students, parents, and staff. I kept every last one of them; they are precious to me. I have included a few at the end of the book so you can read them.

I can't begin to tell you how many times, on my birthday, the students would secretly plan something to surprise me. They would get a big poster board and write sweet notes to me all over it or do other kind and loving things to honor me.

When we would do a drama performance, my arms would be filled with flowers at the curtain. Many students would ask to take pictures with me, and there were always lots of hugs and tears.

While teaching English, I read countless journals and created safe relationships with students where they shared their deepest thoughts. One student moved away, and we continued to send the journal back and forth through the mail.

I've been in touch with one of my former students and his mother since he was in my first drama club in 1985.

I recently reconnected with two former students. One is now married and lives in Napa. She tracked me down and we're in contact. She says she still has her journal from my 7th grade English class. The other student was in my first year of teaching in 1985-86. We kept in contact for several years but eventually lost touch. Come to find out she had been searching for me ever since and found me through the Internet. She is now married with children of her own. During our communication, she mentioned how important the journal was to her; it created a safe place for her to voice her concerns.

I had a student in drama who was so afraid to perform. He finally got up the courage to do "Sandy" from "Grease" for our lip sync show. He was so proud of this, a few years later while he was in high school, he brought his girlfriend in to see the video of our lip sync show. Years later he emailed me to tell me how much the lip sync show changed his life.

I have countless relationships with former students. One of my students was in my drama class for 6th, 7th, and 8th grades. When she got to high school, she came back and helped my costumer. Later, when my main costumer went to work at another school, she became my full time costumer for our yearly productions, even though she lives in Las Vegas. She now works at Cirque du Soleil and was my costumer until I retired. My last show, she came with her three week old baby.

Another former student is a singer in New York City, and we have stayed in touch. She wrote one of the beautiful letters that I have in my cherished binder.

Before dress rehearsal of our final show, I was taken into the prop room, where hand props and costumes were kept, to reveal that my coaches had placed a plaque dedicating the room to me. I stood sobbing while students all looked at me while they sang "Just the Way You Are" by Bruno Mars. At my final drama performances, current and former students wrote tributes to me that were read at the curtain or written in a book. Our superintendent, PK Diffenbaugh, got up on stage after our last performance, and announced that the Colton stage would henceforth be called "The Victoria Lucido Stage." It was my dream come true to have the stage named for me. The fact that it happened before I retired was such an honor since many dedications happen after the person is deceased. His daughter was one of my star drama students and, she, along with her father and her mother, Vanessa Diffenbaugh, offered tremendous support to me and the drama program.

I was often honored by staff members too. My last day of school before retiring was one of the best days of my life because all day long there were gifts and speeches. Each department created singing telegrams to run in and sing to me while I was running my final talent show. I sang "My Way" to my final audience. While I was setting up Karaoke for our end of the year carnival, I was called outside and my students were lined up with flowers to hand to me. I walked through them while they sang "Give my Regards to Broadway."

Recently I received a call from a former student's parent. His daughter, who was in what I call my "Drama Hall of Fame," passed away at the young age of thirty-three-years old. Her father called to tell me about the impact I had on her life. I can't imagine a more meaningful honor.

There are so many other stories of the abundance of rewards I received from students, parents, and staff. I learned early on, however, you can never expect a reward. You have to do your job and believe it is usually reward enough. Any more is icing on the cake. There were years when I was showered with Holiday gifts from students, and there were years when I could count the gifts on one hand. Those gifts can be stressful for teachers because when students don't offer anything, you wonder if you're where you should be. I had to learn not to take the amount of gifts from students personally.

I'm in no way bragging when I write about the gifts I received. I just want you to know there are rewards out there. You can't expect them, and you will often be surprised by how they come to you. If you work hard, give of yourself, and do your best to love and teach the students, I believe rewards in many forms will come to you.

Final Thoughts

Writing this book has really helped me to process my years of experience in education. It's interesting to me because, for 33 years I honed my skills as a teacher, and then, poof, it's over! I learned so much while on the job; I decided to share it with others. I would like to make someone else's teaching life a little easier by offering insights from my experience.

I said in the beginning of the book, while reading this, you may think, "Geez, did she even like to teach?" I hope my love of teaching came through, even though I realize I did not sugar-coat my words. It was important for me to "tell it like it is." Your experience may be entirely different. All I can do is speak from what was true for me. Many books I read have a rather Pollyanna approach to teaching, and then one gets in the classroom and thinks, "What the heck? No one ever told me about this in college." My book is designed to prepare you for those untold experiences.

One thing I loved about teaching was I could bring my entire authentic self to the classroom. I didn't have to pretend I was something I wasn't. When I worked in the bank, I felt I had to put on a "professional banking face." I suppose it was one aspect of my personality, but with teaching, I could bring in most all aspects.

Another thing I loved about teaching was the students were 100% authentic. There may have been a lot of bureaucracy with the district office and the administration but not with the kids. Now, of course, they could drive you crazy at times, but they were real, and I always loved that about them. I often felt the district office focused on the business of education. They would say they were doing whatever for the kids, but to me, it seemed many of their decisions were based in large part on money. I get that. We have to stay afloat financially. As a teacher, it wasn't about money or business, it was about the kids. I was on the frontline with them, and I gave it all I had with my whole heart and soul. Sometimes my best was better than other times, but I always tried my hardest to do a good job.

Through the years, people would say to me, kids are so different now, aren't they? The truth is, kids are kids. Yes, technology has changed and they are affected by it. The world seems to be speeding up, and social media contributes in a big way. What hasn't changed is what hasn't changed for all of us. It's like Maslow's Hierarchy I learned about in college. We are all human beings with feelings and needs the same as the first people who walked the planet.

So, while students may have shorter attention spans or be able to better navigate technology, they still want to have their basic needs met. Kids want to have friends, they want to belong, they want to feel safe, and they want to know they are seen, heard, and accepted.

Those things were important to me when I was a kid (and even now). They were important to kids when I first started teaching and they will always be important. In those ways, kids are still the same.

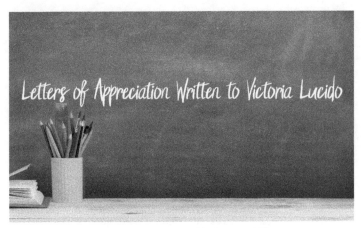

Letters of Appreciation Written to Victoria Lucido

Walter Colton Middle School PTA
Letter of Excellence

April 13, 1994

Dear Vickie ,

The Colton PTA along with Bess Halley would like to express its thanks to you for all the help you have given the students during the current school year. No one faculty member has an exclusive on the word "teaching"; the whole staff is involved. As part of that team, your effort has been extraordinary; you have often gone far beyond the call of duty.

We especially want to commend you for your participation in:

- drama productions
- arranging Phatom of the Opera field trip
- singing telegrams
-school spirit lip sync shows
- talent shows in class
-costumes for Halloween

You also have counseled them as teacher, coach, advisor, and friend.

You know how hard you have worked. We know, too.

Sincerely,

Patti Hagio

Patti Hagio
Colton Middle School PTA
President

129

Dear Mrs. Lucido,

Thank you for being such a wonderful teacher. It has been such a privilege to have you teach me. Hopefully I will be fortunate enough to have a teacher as fantastic as you in years to come. I want you to know that being a teacher is one of the most rewarding jobs you could ever have.

Thank you for showing caring and respect towards everyone. Whenever a student has an issue, you help them with it. You treat every student as an individual and as an equal. You give kids a great, comfortable teaching environment and I thank you for that.

Thank you for your devotion and effort you put into everything you do. This school wouldn't be the same if you didn't put as much hard work you do to make every performance the best it can be. You put out all your energy to make everything a little more than perfect, and we're all thankful.

Thank you for being so creative and making every class activity a fun one. You don't know how many times I have laughed in your class and said that I can't wait for my Drama class. I honestly hope that in the future I will have a class as fun, entertaining, and as educational as one like yours. Thank you for being a teacher that could never be replaced.

Sincerely,

Victoria
Walter Colton Leadership class

Dear Mrs. Lucido,

Thank you for everything you have taught me. Since the day I got here last year you have been so kind. Not only in Social Studies where you taught me about the past, but also in drama where you taught me, along with around forty others, all of the wonderful things we could do in the future. You also showed us to simply be confident in places or situations we are new to.

You gave everyone a safe environment to act and to be comfortable in. Many people found their friends in drama class, like me.

You've stayed at Walter Colton long enough for me to be able to meet you, and I'm so grateful that I did! I will miss you so much when I move. I know tons of your drama students moving on to the ninth grade will come and visit you.

Hopefully there will be two little girls who sit in your class during break just like Kimi and me. When you need something I hope they will be the first to raise their hands.

I hope you have a fantastic birthday and love everything a few of us have planned for you!

♥ ERIN

Vickie,

As we all know, you have a deep love for animals, especially wild animals. Justine mentioned to me that wolves are actually your favorite, and we wondered what it was that draws you to wolves over some of the other animals. So we did a little research, and we think we understand now, for you have many similar qualities.

To begin, wolves are famous for their legendary howling, which they use effectively to communicate. Like the wolf, you have a beautifully distinct voice that compels people to listen to you.

In addition, wolves are committed to their pack and are known to develop close relationships and strong social bonds. We have all benefited from your lasting, 27 year commitment to your Colton pack.

And finally, wolves are fiercely protective of their young, just as you have been fiercely protective of Colton - anyone outside of our Colton family who has made the mistake of criticizing Colton in front of you has certainly been firmly and fiercely corrected.

With this in mind, Justine and I want to present this gift which was actually created by a Colton student. We hope that you will enjoy this as a memento of your wild days leading our pack at Colton!

With love,

Justine and Sherry

I have a lifetime of people to thank for my 33 years of experience in education which enabled me to write *Classroom Confidential*. There are countless students, parents, school staff, community members, district employees, administrators, and superintendents who have worked alongside me every step of my career. I learned from each and every one of them. But since it is impossible to name all of the people who had an effect on me while I was teaching, I would like to begin by thanking the Monterey Peninsula Unified School District. I was a student there from kindergarten through 12th grade and ended up teaching there for my entire career. I have appreciated being able to work in the community that means so much to me.

Next I would like to thank my Walter Colton Middle School family. After working at Fitch Middle School for six years, I ended up at Colton for the next 27. Colton was my home away from home and I appreciate all of the people connected with

Colton all of those years who enriched my life and taught me so much. And in particular, I would like to thank Kim Kellam, Marianne Hartfelt, Alyssa Grainger, and Janet Mikkelsen. Those Colts all agreed to read my manuscript and write a recommendation, a foreword, or, in Alyssa's case, spend countless hours doing one more line edit job. Thank you for your time, support, and encouragement, Ladies!

I would like to thank my brother, Robert Minearo, who has always encouraged me to use my experience in creative ways, beginning with my one-woman-show *Pretty* and then with writing my book. I also want to thank Robert for suggesting the title *Classroom Confidential*. Thank you to my sister, Becky Venard, who read my book and offered words of wisdom and encouragement which kept me going.

My friend Shelley Wise helped by introducing me to my editor Marcia Rosen. I am beyond grateful for Marcia's expertise, her patience, her knowledge, and her belief in me. I never could have gotten to where I am today with *Classroom Confidential* without her.

A big thank you to Margaret "Margie" Dorsett at Copy King, our full-service copy center here in Monterey. Margie has helped with my manuscript in a myriad of different ways.

I would like to sincerely thank all of the staff at Morgan James Publishing beginning with Dave Sauer, the literary scout for Morgan James who first contacted me to discuss my vision for *Classroom Confidential*. I was really nervous to speak with him, but he was so friendly and supportive, which helped me to relax and truly enjoy our conversation. I'm also grateful for the author support team, who guided me through the first steps,

David Hancock the Founder of Morgan James, who chose to take a chance on me, Jim Howard the Publishing Director, who was so kind to me during the Mastermind meeting, and Bonnie Rauch my Author Relations Manager, who guided me through to the final stages of publishing.

Lastly, I would like to thank my family. My stepchildren Anna and Frank 111 Lucido have been excited and supportive of this adventure I'm taking with *Classroom Confidential.* My son Brice Albert has been a huge support and an inspiration to me. Last but certainly not least, I want to extend the deepest thanks to my husband, Frank, who has stood beside me through every project I have undertaken. He is my life partner in every sense of the word.

About the Author: Street Cred

Vickie is a product of the Monterey Peninsula Unified School District and taught there for 33 years. In addition to a Bachelor's in English from San Jose State University, Vickie graduated with a Master of Education from the University of New England.

She has been recognized by "Who's Who of American Teachers" seven times, was awarded "Monterey Teacher of the Year" in 1999 by Monterey Rotary, received the "Mildred Willemsen Award for Excellence in Teaching" in 2011, and was named an" Art Hero" by the Monterey County Office of Education in 2018. Vickie also wrote, directed, and performed in her own one-woman-show *Pretty*.

Upon retirement in 2018, the Colton Middle School Stage was dedicated to her by superintendent PK Diffenbaugh and is now called the "Victoria Lucido Stage."

Vickie lives on the Monterey Peninsula with her husband, Frank, and her two cats Boots and Rocky.

Vickie would love to hear from you. You can connect with her by contacting her through her website at Victorialucidobooks.com